635

Ideas for Social Action

IDEAS FOR SOCIAL ACTION

by
Anthony Campolo

Edited by Wayne Rice

**Additional Material Written by
Wayne Rice and Bill McNabb**

Youth Specialties

Youth Specialties is an imprint of Zondervan
Publishing House, 1415 Lake Drive, S.E.,
Grand Rapids, Michigan 49506

Library of Congress Cataloging in Publication Data

Campolo, Anthony.
    Ideas for social action.
    Originally published: El Cajon, Calif.:
Youth Specialties, c1983.
    Bibliography: p.
    1. Church group work with youth. 2. Church and social problems.
3. Social action. I. Rice, Wayne. II. McNabb, Bill. III. Title.
BV4447.C36 1984   259'.2   84-11876
ISBN 0-310-45251-1 (pbk.)

The pronouns *he/him* and *she/her* are frequently used generically and interchangeably in this book.

Contents

Preface

Several years ago, Tony Campolo, speaking to the National Youth Workers Convention, made a statement that went something like this: "One thing we don't need are more idea books full of games and silly social activities for youth groups! What we need is an idea book on Christian social action!"

This statement was followed by enthusiastic applause from the audience.

Well, we at Youth Specialties must admit that we are still publishing idea books full of games and silly social activities. But we did get the message.

This book is the one that Tony and many other people have wanted to see in print for a long time. We are very proud to be able to offer it to you.

Not all of the ideas in this book are original with Tony or with us. We gathered many of them from a number of sources, including past editions of the *Ideas* library. Although they go unnamed, we'd like to thank all the creative people who came up with these ideas, put them into practice, and then graciously shared what they were doing with us. We especially want to thank Bill McNabb, Von Trutschler, Ken Shea, Chuck Workman, Peggy Campolo, Ron Sider, Jerry Krellwitz, and Jenny Offner for their contributions to this book.

All of the royalties from the sale of this book will be donated to the Evangelical Association for the Promotion of Education to care for and to feed the children at Centre Siloe orphanage and school in Cap Haitian, Haiti. We dedicate this book to a dedicated Haitian pastor, Rev. Mariot Valcin.

—Wayne Rice

Chapter One

The Challenge of Social Action

by Anthony Campolo

Recently I discussed with a local pastor the ministry which his church has had with young people. He was frustrated and discouraged because his church did not seem to be able to hold onto its youth in spite of a host of efforts. His church supported parties, concerts, camping trips, and a variety of other activities aimed at enticing young people and getting their support. Nothing his church did achieved the desired results. In exasperation, he threw up his hands and asked, "What do we have to do for young people in order to attract them?"

"Perhaps," I said, "young people are not attracted so much by a church that tries to entertain them as they are attracted to a church that challenges them to do things for others. If your church provided concrete ways for young people to minister to the needs of others and to effect social change in the world, they would find your church very attractive. Young people just may be looking for a church that appeals to their latent idealism by calling them to be agents of God's revolution and to be part of His movement to bring healing and justice to His broken world." I believe that the church that calls young people to engage in ministry to the community by helping the poor, working for racial equality, caring for the elderly, and improving life for the disadvantaged, will find that it will attract numerous young people who are looking for the fulfillment that comes from investing their lives in the service of others.

As a college teacher, I have had the opportunity to spearhead social action programs on the campus. These efforts have ranged from attempts to secure better living conditions for migrant workers to a program aimed at planned racial segregation of housing. Time and time again, I have found myself surrounded by some of the brightest student leaders in the school. They were interested in participating in social action programs and, in more cases than not, these social action programs led these students to a deeper commitment to Jesus Christ. They were attracted by a Christianity that was different from the "pie in the sky when you die" variety. They were attracted by a form of Christianity that found in Christ an imperative to improve society and utilize the Bible to develop principles of social action.

A church which provides its young people with opportunities and challenges for social change gives to them the opportunity to explore some of the primary reasons for their salvation. Through these activities they will come to see that Jesus is not only interested in saving them from sin and getting them into heaven, but also wants to make them into instruments through which He can do His work in the world. They will come to see that God not only wants His people to reign with Him in glory after death, but that in the midst of this life He wants them to be the instruments through which He ministers to the needs of the downtrodden and effects social justice. Young people involved in social action will come to understand that God is infinitely concerned with what happens to refugees from Cambodia, the isolated elderly in urban high-rise apartments, the derelicts on skid row, the poor in Appalachia, and the victims of racial segregation. They will come to know a God who is angry when a multinational corporation pursues exploitive policies in a Third World nation, or when politicians promote policies which serve special interest groups at the expense of the poor. They would come to understand that God is One who is joyful when there are opportunities for oppressed people to gain dignity. In short, social action programs help young people to understand something of the nature of God and to gain an understanding of why God chose to save them from sin and make them into new creatures.

Jesus Came to Transform Society

It is a mistake to think that Jesus was only interested in saving individuals so that they could go to heaven when they died. Jesus broke into history with a declaration that He had come to initiate the Kingdom of God. Many of His parables were given to teach us some of the principles upon which this kingdom was to be developed. The Sermon on the Mount provided the ethic for this kingdom. When Jesus taught us how to pray He encouraged us to yearn that the kingdom might exist on earth as it already exists in heaven.

The kingdom which Jesus initiated is a new social order composed of people who are obedient to the will of God, who structure their lives and their social institutions in accord with His desires and maintain a system of human relationships that reflect His love and justice. *Jesus wants to create a revolutionary new society.* Once we grasp that, we can begin to understand why He was crucified. The custodians of the status quo, who had a vested interest in maintaining the established social order with all of its oppression and injustice, predictably opposed this man who called for the creation of a new regime. While His adversaries may have been blind to the fact that Jesus was the Son of God, they clearly recognized that He was socially dangerous. The accusations that they leveled at Him as He moved toward the crucifixion expressed their fear of Him. They said, "He stirreth up the people," and that "It is necessary for this man to die, that Israel (the established social order) might be saved."

There are some who try to suggest that Jesus was nailed to the cross because He preached peace and love and told people to be kind to each other. This opinion ignores the fact that talk of peace and love does not get you crucified: it gets you a speaking engagement at the local Rotary Club. It was because the doctrine propagated by Jesus necessitated a new and just socio-economic order that those who had a vested interest in the status quo sought to do away with Him.

I am not attempting to reduce Christianity to some simplistic social Gospel. God's kingdom does not become a reality simply by facilitating a few positive social changes with the expectation that all will be well if we can just eliminate corrupt institutional structures. On the contrary, there will be no kingdom unless it is populated by people who incarnate the nature and the values of the King. This can't happen until the King transforms them into His character and likeness. People need to be saved from sin. They need to be converted. They need to be made into new creatures. Transformations in the lives of individuals are essential before we can have the kind of people who can effect the institutional changes which are essential if the kingdom is to come "on earth as it is in heaven."

Jesus calls us to move beyond a desire for personal piety to a desire to serve others, especially those who are desperately poor. The contrast between these two emphases became brilliantly clear to me as the result of hearing a bright student deliver a talk at a Christian college chapel service. He opened by saying, "Last night, according to U.N. statistics, approximately ten thousand people starved to death. Furthermore, most of you don't give a shit. What is worse, most of you are more upset with the fact that I just said "shit" than you are over the fact that ten thousand people starved to death last night. That's what I want to talk to you about —your morality."

There is no doubt in my mind that to be a Christian is to have your heart broken by the things that break the heart of God. To be a Christian is to be filled with righteous indignation over the fact that we affluent Americans live with a high level of indifference to the unjust privations of people around the world. The Jesus of Scripture beckons us to change a world in which 500 million people suffer from malnutrition while the rich in other nations suffer from overweight. He calls us to transform it into a world in which the needs of all people are satisfied.

I was once with a group of students who had just completed a month of exhausting labor rebuilding a Third World village which had been destroyed by a hurricane. On the day we were to leave the village the people threw a party for us. There was singing and dancing. Laughter abounded everywhere. As I stood at the edge of the party, looking on with pleasure and satisfaction, an old man of the village pulled me aside and said, "You can tell me now. You're a Communist, aren't you? You and your friends are Communists. Right?"

I said, "No, of course not. I oppose Communism. I'm a Christian. What makes you think that I or my students are Communists?"

He said, "You care about poor people."

His response upset me more than I can say. Why should the Communists have the reputation of caring about people? Why aren't

Christians known as the ones who are most concerned about the poor and the oppressed people of the world? Perhaps it's because we haven't been the most concerned.

Peter Berger, the sociologist, claims that the future of the world belongs to that ideology which can provide the most hope for the future. If that is the case, then true Christianity will win out, providing we declare its vision to the world. Romans 8:19-39 tells us that everything and everyone is waiting for the people of God to declare the deliverance and redemption of God.

What we are dealing with here is the purpose of salvation. When Jesus died on the cross, it was not simply to make it possible for us to go to heaven when we die. Jesus saved us in order that He might use us to be the agents through which He can change His world into the kind of world He willed for it to be when He created it. He saved us from sin in order to make us into visible agents of His revolution. He wanted to make us into the kind of people through whom His reign might begin to be a reality in human history.

This new society is His to create. It will not be ushered in through our efforts. Actually, the Kingdom of God will never become a complete social, historical reality until the Lord Himself returns at the *eschaton.* The point that is being made is that God started to bring His kingdom into being through Christ; He continues to build it through us and will bring it to completeness and fulfillment at the day of His coming. However, the kingdom that will be is even now in the process of being created, and He has given us the privilege of becoming instruments through which His kingdom, in all of its personal and social ramifications, is being unravelled in our time.

In summary, let me simply say that God's will is to establish His kingdom on earth just as it is in heaven and that He has called us to join Him in this great task. Our responsibility is to win people to Jesus, to enlist them in this cause and to join together with Him and His disciples in changing every social practice and institution into what God wills for it to be.

A Dream for the Church

In Wayne, Pennsylvania, there is a church which during the civil rights era mortgaged its building for $100,000. It wanted money, not to build an addition to its educational facilities (as is usually the case), but to give to creative projects in the black community. This church helped establish day-care centers in the ghetto, job-training programs for the underprivileged and unemployed, tutoring programs for struggling teenagers, and drug rehabilitation centers. People were shocked at the action of this church. Newspapers wrote stories on it. The pastor was interviewed on television and talk shows. The church was the talk of the town. Why? Because that church dared to restructure itself for service to the world instead of being structured for its own survival.

We need a Church that will do what God created it to do. We need a Church that is willing to divest itself of wealth, power and prestige for the sake of the poor and distraught. We need a Church which will imitate its Founder and adopt the role of the Suffering Servant.

When it comes to restructuring the Church, I have a dream. I long for a Church organized in small cellular units of four or five members. I see each of these groups committed to some special mission in the world. For example, one group would work for better schools, another to end the abuses of the multinational corporations in Third World nations, another to better the condition of the elderly, another to save the environment, another to support missions, and all of them would be committed to winning new converts to Christ. The list could go on, describing thousands of small groups, each striving to change the world into the Kingdom of God. There would be a pastor, but his job would be far different from that of the typical clergy. The pastor would be a resource person for these groups. He would help them understand what the Bible has to say about what they are trying to accomplish and the ways in which they should proceed. This pastor would facilitate the formation of new groups, and teach the members how to grow in love towards each other.

The laity would realize their true potential through the action of these groups. Laypeople would no longer be second-class Christians whose only purpose is to support the clergy in their ministry. Instead, the laity would be viewed as the real ministers of the Gospel, and the clergy would be viewed as persons called to equip these saints to fulfill their calling. Thus, Biblically prescribed roles would be realized:

> And he gave some apostles; and some, prophets; and some, evangelists; and some, pastors and teachers; for the perfecting of the

saints for the work of the ministry. (Eph. 4:11,12a KJV)

Because these small groups would be committed to changing the world, they would have to engage in intensive Bible study. Their members would come to realize that the Scriptures are not meant to be simply devotional material to inspire them through a day's work. Instead, they would look to the Bible as the ultimate source for developing the strategy of their revolution. The Bible would provide the methodology they would employ in bringing about social change; it would establish the ethical conditions for social action, and it would enable the participants in God's revolution to know what to expect. Armed with Scripture, they would not be discouraged when their efforts seemed fruitless or when they were ridiculed or persecuted. They would know that they labored in the hope and faith that all things will work together for good and that God who has begun a good work in them will complete it on the day of the Second Coming.

Prayer meetings would be times of deep encounter with the Holy Spirit. In these small groups, members would help each other to discover their spiritual gifts. Christians, often unaware of the talents and gifts which the Spirit has given them, would discover through the perceptions of their brothers and sisters in Christ those things which God has equipped them to do. Unlike so many who cannot see what God has called them to do and be, the members of these groups would be submissive to each other and discover through their mutual fellowship the nature of God's calling. The extreme individualism encouraged by the American culture would be replaced by a community of believers through which the Holy Spirit could reveal His will.

There would be much to pray about when these groups assembled. Their members would call upon the Lord to direct their plans and guide them in the development of strategy. They would know that without dependence upon the Holy Spirit they could easily end up in misguided efforts to facilitate social change which would cause more damage than good. They would pray for courage to carry out their plans. They would look to God for help when they encountered barriers and opposition to their efforts to do His will. They would pray for their enemies and seek God's grace to enable them to be redemptive toward those who oppose His will.

Prayer and Bible study groups generally fail to live up to expectations because they exist primarily for the edification of their members. These groups would be different. They would exist for deployment in the world. Their reason to exist would be to change the world. Their times of prayer and Bible study would equip them to carry out their missions in society. Their vitality would result from giving away their lives for the sake of the Gospel and for the sake of the world.

These groups would be effective instruments for bringing about social change because they would be in the world. There would be Christian union members in one group endeavoring to discover ways to make their union into what God intended for it to be. There would be corporate executives meeting for prayer and Bible study in order to learn how they could be transformers, even within their companies. There would be teen-agers meeting together to discern ways of Christianizing their high school.

Each Sunday these groups would join together for corporate worship. The worship services would be different from what is typical in most churches. Each group would tell what it was doing, what God had accomplished through its efforts and how persons had been evangelized through its message. As each report was given, other groups would sing for joy because of what God was doing. They would be filled with praise for the One who is directing the revolution. They would sing of the kingdom which was breaking loose in history.

This is a dream. But it is a dream that can become a reality. A youth group can be the first such cellular unit through which a new kind of church might begin to emerge. Through such a humble beginning a new structure for the church could develop.

The Biblical Prescription for Social Action

The idea that the church is called to transform the world is not a new concept. Certainly, theologians since Calvin have made this mission an important part of their message. However, theologians often fail to give a Biblical prescription as to how we are to go about carrying out this imperative. Usually we Christians end up adopting very "worldly" ways for effecting social change. We resort to the use of power.

In 1976, I was a Democratic candidate for the U.S. Congress. I had a very simple understanding of what was wrong with America and how to straighten out the whole mess. The nation was ruled by bad guys and all that was necessary to set things right was to elect good guys to take their places. If good guys held the power then all would be well. However, I failed to ask the very simple question, "What made the bad guys bad?" If I had, I might have concluded that part of the reason was the fact that they possessed power.

People with power quickly discover that there is only one way to hold on to it — through compromise. The maintenance of political power requires that those who hold it give in to the demands of a variety of special interest groups. The capitulation to their demands need not be total, but there must be some yielding in order to mollify them. Only the powerless can afford to be direct and consistent as they speak out on the controversial iusses — they have nothing to lose.

Power and authority are opposite ends of a continuum. Power is the ability to *make* others do your will, even if it is contrary to their own. Authority is the ability to persuade others to *want* to do your will and to desire the things that you want. There is a tendency for authority to decrease as power increases. On the other hand, as your authority increases it becomes less and less necessary to depend upon power in order to get people to do your will.

As we consider the differences between authority and power it becomes obvious that Jesus spoke with authority rather than forcing His will upon us by the use of power. He did not try to change us by demanding that we obey Him, even if obedience was against our wills. Instead, He endeavored to win us to Himself so that we would do His bidding out of love. When He entered history He did not come with a marching army forcing us into submission. Rather, He came as a powerless baby in a manger drawing us to Him in a non-threatening manner. He would not force us to our knees as oppressed slaves to His dictates, but ultimately would present Himself to us on a cross, declaring that "If I be lifted up I will draw all men unto myself." History attests to the fact that the authority of the cross has been a more effective means of influencing men and establishing lordship over them than have all the armies that have ever marched and all the laws that have ever been passed.

17

When Jesus entered history He divested Himself of power and, in accord with the fifty-third chapter of Isaiah, became a suffering servant. He set aside the glory that would dazzle men into submission and came to us in humility. The great Christological passage of Scripture in Philippians 2:5-11 reads:

> Have this attitude in yourselves which was also in Christ Jesus, who, although He existed in the form of God, did not regard equality with God a thing to be grasped, but emptied Himself, taking the form of a bond-servant, and being made in the likeness of men. And being found in appearance as a man, He humbled Himself by becoming obedient to the point of death, even death on a cross. Therefore also God highly exalted Him, and bestowed on Him the name which is above every name, that at the name of Jesus every knee should bow, of those who are in heaven, and on earth, and under the earth, and that every tongue should confess that Jesus Christ is Lord, to the glory of God the Father. (NASB)

Jesus ultimately established His authority through His death on the cross. By means of sacrificial self-giving He drew men and women Himself. Because of the way in which He gave Himself, people bend their knees to Him and acknowledge Him as Lord. Authority is built on servanthood.

Mother Teresa understood this truth and imitated the life style of Jesus. She emptied herself of wealth, power and prestige and she became a humble servant of the dying poor of India. She gave of herself until there was nothing left to give, and thus she has earned authority that causes the world to listen. What she has to say is listened to by people around the world, not because she commands an army, but because she has earned the right to be heard.

To the worldly, the way of Jesus seems like foolishness. They believe that only the powerful can bring about social change. They think that the powerless count for nothing. But the Bible reminds us that it is through the powerless that the works of the powerful are brought to nothing.

Martin Luther King understood this Biblical principle and used it well. He and his followers marched from Selma to Montgomery as they struggled to bring about equality between the races. On the march they confronted Sheriff Clark and his deputies at the famous bridge outside Selma. Clark told King and his followers to turn back but King responded, "We've come too far to turn back now." King told his people to get down on their knees and pray, and while they were kneeling the sheriff attacked them, bashing their heads with billy clubs. The world shuddered at the scene as it was viewed on live television, and immediately we knew that King's cause had triumphed. The powerless, beaten followers of King were victorious that day while the sheriff with his deputies and power was the loser. After that confrontation, there was no question that the Civil Rights Bill would be passed. The blood of King and his followers had earned the victory. The powerless had triumphed, the lowly had been lifted up and the powerful had been brought down, just as predicted in the first chapter of the Gospel of Luke.

In my own efforts to bring about social change I have witnessed the effectiveness of powerlessness. Some of my students and I joined with two major religious organizations to oppose the role of one of the world's largest multinational corporations in the Dominican Republic. We accused them of growing sugar on land which would be better used to grow food for the hungry Dominicans. We condemned them for not being responsive to the needs of the Dominican people, claiming that they did not provide adequate housing and services for the thousands of workers they employed. We showed up at the stockholders meetings of the corporation and supported resolutions condemning company practices. In all of these condemnations and efforts we accomplished nothing. Eventually we abandoned these tactics realizing that the corporation was far too powerful to be intimidated by a few crusaders who held a few shares of stock. Little by little we ended our confrontational strategy and entered into a cooperative relationship. The leaders of the corporation surprised us. What we could never have forced them to do, they did willingly. They committed $100 million to the social and economic development of the Dominican Republic. The company is building schools, developing medical programs, constructing homes for their workers and making land that formerly grew sugar available to grow crops for indigenous consumption.

In its earliest days Christianity was a healthy, vital movement. It was marked with integrity and was able to challenge the power of Rome through the sufferings of its martyrs. Then in the year 312, everything began to change. Constantine issued the Edict of Milan and Christianity was allied with the power of Caesar. No longer would Christianity be the faith of a persecuted minority. Suddenly Christianity had become the majority. The armies of Rome would establish Christian morality throughout the empire. Society would be forced to yield to Christian law. History attests to the fact that the consequence of this edict was the corruption of the Church and perhaps the weakening of the empire. Time and time again since the time of Constantine the Church has been corrupted when it took on temporal power. It has allied itself with crusading armies, elected rulers to do its bidding and baptized wars and called them holy. In case after case, Christianity betrayed its Founder by these actions and compromised its testimony before those who were not in harmony with its beliefs. When I react negatively to groups like the "Moral Majority" in the twentieth century, it is not because of differences with its members on the issues which they raise; rather, it is because of their grasping for power. Only God has the character to possess power without being corrupted by it.

There may be times when Christians find themselves forced to use power to fight evil. Dietrich Bonhoeffer found it necessary to do so in his opposition of Hitler. But whenever power is assumed, there is a loss of purity, a loss of innocence, and an ambiguous morality is evident. Perhaps as Soren Kierkegaard claims, there come rare moments when there must be a "teleological suspension of the ethical." Generally, however, Christians should challenge the world, not with a sword, but with a cross.

Some of the ideas for social action suggested in this book will not seem far-reaching. Many of the projects will be viewed as being of little consequence in the broad scheme of human events. However, we are part of what Tom Sine has called "The Mustard Seed Conspiracy." We believe that through acts of sacrificial service, the structure of society is changed. We believe that even a "cup of cool water" given in the name of Christ has its reward. We are convinced that the suffering servant will triumph. Though our powerlessness may be ridiculed by a world that thinks in terms of power, we know that it is through what appears as foolishness that the kingdom comes. Please do not view the suggestions in this book as cute activities to occupy the attention of a restless youth group. It is through ideas like these that the world can see a glimpse of what the Kingdom of God is all about.

Chapter Two

Preparing for Social Action

by Wayne Rice

Mission and service projects normally require a great deal of planning and preparation. While Christians need to be prepared to respond immediately whenever they see people who are in great need, Christian social action is not characteristically impulsive or reactionary. Responsible Christian service is carefully planned, well thought out and properly motivated. Everyone involved will know what the needs are, why they are involved, what they hope to accomplish, and exactly how they will go about accomplishing it. It is possible for a youth group, no matter how well-intentioned it may be, to do more harm than good when the members of the group are not properly prepared for the project. Many of the projects in this book can be accomplished in a day or less, but to be done successfully, they may need several weeks of planning and preparation.

This brief chapter is designed to give you some guidelines and suggestions for maximizing the effectiveness of the social action project that you choose to do with your youth group.

The Importance of Leadership

Be sure you have good adult leadership for your project. Leadership is the key. Young people will get very excited about service if their leaders are able to motivate them and show them how it is done. Young people are rarely capable of planning and doing service projects entirely on their own. A good adult-to-teen ratio is about one adult for every eight young people. It is difficult to provide good supervision and guidance for more than that. Before you begin planning your project, determine whether or not your leadership is going to be adequate.

Once you know who your leaders are, it is crucial that they fully understand the scope of the project and be convinced of its importance. Their enthusiasm and confidence will be contagious to the group. If, for example, the proposed project is working in a convalescent hospital, the leaders should visit the hospital first and find out what needs to be done and how it can be done. If the proposed project involves talking to the patients, reading to them, and so on, then the leaders should first do this themselves. Perhaps they could go to the hospital on a regular basis for a few weeks, get to know the staff and some of the patients, and experience for themselves how to serve by serving.

E. G. Von Trutschler (Pastor "Von") of San Diego, an experienced youth worker who has taken hundreds of young people into Mexico and South America to serve the poor, says this: "I would never think of leading kids somewhere I've never been. No way. It destroys your credibility. You need more than words. You've got to be able to say to kids, 'Here's what we're going to do and I'll show you how.' You can't be a leader the first time. You will need to go first, analyze the territory, get to know the people, find out what needs to be done, and then say to the kids, 'follow me.' There may be times when the leaders will have to learn the ropes right along with the kids, but it is generally true that your leaders will be more effective if they can lead from their own experience.

Motivating the Group

A service project needs to be more than just another activity or program on your youth group's calendar. It should be a natural response to the call of Christ to be "doers of the word and not hearers only." Ideally, you will want young people to see social action as a concrete way for them to put their faith into meaningful action, not just a way to have fun, get away from home, be with friends, and so on, although all of those may be involved to some extent. It is impossible, of course, to be sure that everyone will have "pure" motives, but there are a few things you can do that will help the group to understand why social action is so important.

One good approach is to make service the result of Bible study. Most youth groups are involved in regular Bible study of some kind and a service project may be a logical way to apply that which is being learned.

A youth group in Florida, for example, spent several weeks studying the healing ministry of Jesus. They observed how Jesus went out of his way to minister to people whom others had labeled as misfits or "unclean" because of their physical limitations or infirmities. They began to empathize with these people and to feel some of the same kind of compassion that Jesus must have felt. As a result of this study, they started a regular ministry of their own to handicapped and disabled young people in their community. Each week they would bring handicapped youth to their youth meetings and include them in all their activities. This outstanding ministry simply flowed out of their study of Scripture and their desire to do something with what they had learned.

Young people need to get into the habit of seeing Scripture as more than just ancient history or wise and wonderful sayings that they "hide in their hearts." They need to see that the Bible leads us to action and makes a difference in how we live. If we take God's word seriously, it means that we must respond in some way. In many cases, a service project is an excellent way to respond.

You may want to use a Bible study as a way to prepare for a service project that has already been chosen, like a fund-raiser for world hunger relief. In that case, you may want to conduct a Bible study for the purpose of giving the project a solid Biblical base. This is a good way to help young people see the significance of the project.

Another way to sensitize the group and to motivate them to service is to take them out of their comfortable environments and simply let them see for themselves people who are in great need. Pastor Von takes groups of young people to the poorer areas of Mexico on field trips, not to do anything, but to just observe. "I want the kids to observe and to not feel guilty about just observing," he says. "You don't always have to *do* something." Once young people have seen, heard, smelled, felt, experienced — then they can make some kind of commitment about

"doing something."

You may want to take your group to an orphanage, to a hospital, to a ghetto, to the "red light district," or to any number of places where human need and deprivation exist. Out of such visits, young people may be motivated to return and they will have firsthand knowledge about what needs to be done.

There are also a variety of educational strategies that motivate young people to get involved in Christian social action. These include simulation games, role plays, case studies, media presentations, and similar experiences that help kids learn about things like poverty, racism, war, aging, and the like. Once they learn about a particular need, they can then consider possible responses.

For example, a youth group in California sponsored a "Small World Banquet" and invited everyone from the church to come and enjoy a "unique dining experience" featuring both American and foreign cuisine. When the guests arrived, they were seated randomly at tables representing the various countries of the world: The United States, Japan, Mexico, India, Pakistan, Bangladesh, etc. When the food was served, those seated at tables representing "rich" industrial nations (like the U.S.) received delicious steak dinners with all the trimmings. Those seated at tables representing poorer nations received a small portion of beans, soup, or rice with water. The rich countries were permitted "seconds" but the poor countries were not, because there was barely enough of their food to go around the first time.

Before long, some of the "poor" tables came begging at the "rich" tables, and some became angry with the unfairness of the situation. Soon many of the rich spontaneously began sharing their food with the poor, and before long everyone was satisfied.

Following the meal, a film was shown and a discussion was held concerning world hunger. People felt highly motivated to give out of their abundance so that others might be fed.

Another youth worker used the old Parker Brothers game, "Monopoly," to help the young people learn about poverty and injustice in the world. The group divided into four teams and each team acted as one "player" in the Monopoly game. Two of the teams were given a lot of money to start with and two of the teams were given a very small amount of money. In other words, there were two rich teams and two poor teams.

One of the rich teams was to be a "Christian" team and to play the game according to Christian principles. Likewise, one of the "poor" teams was to be a Christian team. The remaining two teams (one rich and one poor) were to have no religious beliefs at all.

The game was then played using the regular rules, buying and selling property, etc., but with each team making their decisions based upon the economic situation that they were given and their faith and religious values. As the game progressed, the inequalities inherent in the game and the difficulties for survival became apparent. Because the game simulated reality so well, the young people were able to experience frustration, impotence, anger, greed, and other emotions that are caused by an unjust system. It eventually led to the group's involvement in a social action project to help the disadvantaged.

Youth Specialties publishes a number of books called *IDEAS* which contain many ideas like the Small World Banquet and the Monopoly game described here. They can be very useful for motivating young people to become interested in social action and service.

Choosing the Project

There are more than two hundred ideas for social action in this book from which to choose. In addition, there are an infinite number of possibilities for social action that aren't in this or any other book. How do you decide what to do? Obviously, you can't do everything.

Choosing the right project for your group will involve a number of considerations. An obvious one is the group itself. The age of the young people, their abilities, their maturity, their interests — all of these will likely be factors in your choice. If, for example, social action is new to your group, then you may want to begin with something simple like a fund raiser or a canned food drive. But if the group is mature and experienced at doing service projects, then something like "Adopt a Grandparent," a workcamp, or one of the "political" ideas in chapter five might be a good choice.

Another consideration is the area of need or concern about which your group feels most strongly. For example, some groups are concerned about the elderly, others are concerned about injustice, and others are concerned about underprivileged children. These areas of concern may arise out of a Bible study, a field trip, a special speaker, or a film. Your choice of projects will be easier if you know which particular need your group is most inclined to meet.

There are many logistical considerations as well. What can be done in your local area? What resources are available? How much money will it take? How much time? How many leaders do we have? If travel is involved, how can that be arranged? And so forth. Questions like these must have answers before you make a choice. If your group chooses a project but doesn't consider basic logistics, then the results will be frustration and failure.

The following step-by-step process may be helpful for your group in deciding what to do:

1. Determine the area of greatest need. Let the young people make an initial decision concerning the focus of the project: the poor, the sick, refugees, the elderly, peace, civil rights, etc.

2. Brainstorm possible courses of action. Use this book, plus the creative thinking of the group, to make a long list of everything that might be possible to meet the need that you are concerned about. Keep in mind that the first rule of brainstorming is that all ideas are acceptable, no matter how "far out" they may seem.

3. Select from that list the best five or six ideas in terms of their overall impact or their potential for a positive result. Ask, "If we were able to do this, what would be accomplished?"

4. Narrow those down to two or three that your group would be best equipped to do. Here's where all those logistical questions need to be asked. Can we, with the people and resources available to us, actually pull it off?

5. Now, choose one of those and go to it.

Preparing for Social Action

Once you have decided upon a particular project, the actual preparation begins. It would be impossible to suggest here every necessary step in preparation for the project you choose, since every project is unique and will require more or less preparation depending on what it is. There are, however, a few general recommendations that can be made.

First, get the support of the rest of the church. Let the pastor, the church board, the parents, the missions committee — anyone who might be interested — know about the project and get their approval and support. This will usually result in offers of help as well.

Contact the people you want to serve and ask for their permission and advice. If you are going to work in a convalescent home, a rescue mission, an inner-city school, or a retarded children's home, go there and discuss your plans with them. Let them know why the group is coming. Assure them that they will be adequately prepared and will have good adult leadership. Find out if the project can be done in cooperation with them. Maybe the youth group can work alongside the recipients of the project, rather than coming in and doing all the work themselves.

Acquaint the group with the people they will be serving. If, for example, the group is going to work in a retarded children's home, then take the young people on a preliminary visit just to be exposed to the children and their environment. Have someone from the staff of the home come to a youth group meeting to answer questions and to give advice and suggestions on what to do in certain situations. If there are films, books or other resources that might be helpful, use them to prepare the group for what they will encounter during the project itself. If this is not done, there is the danger that some young people will be shocked by what they see and the experience may be a negative one for them.

Make sure each person knows exactly what he or she will be doing. Divide up the responsibilities so that everyone feels involved. Conduct practice sessions or "dry runs" to sharpen the skills that will be needed. If the group is going to be doing construction work, then take a day to teach the group how to drive nails, mix concrete, or hang wallpaper. If the group is going to be doing personal work, like visiting people in the hospital, role-play a variety of situations to gain some valuable experience before the actual project begins.

Preparation will also include acquiring necessary tools, supplies, travel arrangements, insurance, food, lodging, and so forth. Each project will have its own set of details which will need to be taken care of.

Additional Considerations

Before you begin your social action project, there are a number of other important items to consider, such as setting goals. Set goals which are attainable. Don't tackle more than the group can handle. If the

Young people prepare for the mission field by attending a Teen Missions "Boot Camp".

project is a fund raiser, identify a dollar amount which is high enough to motivate the group, but not so high that it will frustrate them or lead them to inevitable failure. If you are washing windows up and down neighborhood streets, decide how many windows, streets or houses you are going to complete. Be reasonable, as it is always better to do *more* than you set out to do than to do less. Your goals should also be communicated to the recipients of the project. They need to know that you are going to do what you said you would do. Don't leave a project half-finished.

Second, help the group to approach the project with humility. It is easy for young people to let pride settle in and for groups to feel that they are "better" than the people to whom they are ministering. Young people should feel proud of their achievements, but they need to understand that service is a privilege and a duty, not a heroic deed or performance that demands applause. There can be no paternalism or arrogance while serving others. An improper attitude can sour the effectiveness of a good social action project.

Third, make your social action project a matter of great prayer. Have your young people pray daily for the project and commit it to the Lord. Help the group to understand that they are not doing the work alone, but that God wants to go with them and wants to bless their efforts. Many young people will feel inadequate for the task, but like Moses, they can go knowing that God will show them what to do and what to say. They must remember to ask God's blessing on what they do.

Finally, plan ahead for how you will de-brief the group. Many groups fail to do this, yet it is a vitally important part of every social action project. Following the project (or during the project if it involves an extended period of time), the group needs to reflect on their experience and to discuss what happened. They need to share their feelings and ask what they learned about themselves, about each other, the needy, their faith, and the gospel. This is where the real pay-off is in social action. We don't serve just to be "do-gooders," but because service is tied inexorably to the meaning of our faith in Christ. We need to take time to think about the implications of what we have done, to allow the Holy Spirit to teach us through the experience and to give thanks for what has been accomplished.

Following almost all of Jesus' public discourses and miracles, the disciples would gather around for a "de-briefing" by Jesus. He never allowed those teachable moments to get away and neither should we.

Another way to follow up the project is to share the experience with the rest of the church. Take pictures, have several young people prepare short talks to give in a church service, or put together an article for the church newsletter. People who supported the project with their prayers or financial gifts need to know how it went.

This book is loaded with great ideas. Hopefully, it will serve to get you excited about Christian social action. Remember that whatever you do, it needs to be carefully planned and carried out so that as an offering of love and as an act of worship, it will be acceptable to our Lord Jesus Christ.

Chapter Three

Service Projects that Meet Special Human Needs

Introduction by Anthony Campolo

The first and best kind of social action is "personalistic" in nature. It is a Christian response to individuals who are in need. It flows with compassion and is a natural style of service for young people who are committed to Christ. There can be no criticism of social action that results in feeding the hungry, clothing the naked, healing the sick, and visiting those who are in prison. Such actions are direct and apolitical. People have needs; Christians become aware of those needs; Christians meet those needs. This is simply doing what Jesus would do. The church is, according to the Scriptures, the Body of Christ—the actual presence of Jesus in the world. As individual members of that Body, we are in fact His hands and His feet—ministering to a broken humanity.

Some years ago I was in the Dominican Republic doing research on missionary work. I had been working in the western part of the country near the Haitian border. Because I was scheduled to be flown back to the capitol city of Santo Domingo in a small Piper Cub, I was waiting for the airplane at the edge of a grass landing strip. As I stood there, a woman approached me. She was carrying her baby in her arms. The child was suffering from malnutrition; its stomach was swollen to four or five times its normal size. Its hair had taken on that rusty tint which is evidence of malnutrition. The pupils in its eyes were rolled back, so that only white showed. The child's arms and legs were as spindly as my thumb. This dying, emaciated child hung limp in its mother's hands as she began to beg me to take him.

She pleaded with me, "Please, mister, take my baby. Don't leave my baby here to die. My boy will die if he stays here. Take my baby. Make him well. Take my baby, mister. Don't leave my baby here to die." I turned away from her and tried to escape her pleadings, but she became all the more insistent. Raising her voice, she shouted at me, "Take my baby. Take my baby. Don't leave my baby to die."

I tried to get away from her, but there was no evading her plea. It went on and on. I was relieved when I saw the airplane come into sight and then land. I ran across the field as quickly as I could to get into the plane and away from her. She came running after me screaming, "Take my baby. Take my baby. Don't leave my baby here to die."

I climbed into the plane and closed the plexiglass door, but she was alongside of the plane, beating on the fuselage, still screaming at the top of her lungs for me to take her child. The pilot started up the engine and the plane pulled away from the woman, down the landing strip, and into the air.

As we circled the field, I could see her solitary figure below. And halfway back to Santo Domingo it dawned on me; I realized who it was that I had left behind on that landing strip. The name of that baby was Jesus; the Jesus who said, "Inasmuch as ye have done it unto the least of these my brethren, ye have done it unto me. And inasmuch as ye have failed to do it unto the least of these my brethren, ye have failed to do it unto me."

Someday when I stand before the Judgement Seat, the Lord will say, "I was hungry and you never fed me, I was naked and you never clothed me, I was sick and you never ministered to me, I was a stranger and you did not take me in."

And I will say, "Lord, when did I see you hungry and not feed you, naked and not clothe you, sick and not minister to you, a stranger and not take you in?"

And the Lord will say, "Just east of the Haitian border, on a landing strip; when you failed to respond to that child, you failed to respond to me."

Everyone who knows the Bible is aware that it teaches that Christians must respond to individuals who are in need whenever such individuals confront them. Even if the needy person is an enemy, we are called to feed him and to treat him with love. The world offers a multitude of opportunities to serve Christ by serving desperate people. There are elderly people who live lonely and estranged lives in county homes for the aged. When we lovingly visit them we are visiting Christ. There are hungry people in Haiti, and Bangladesh, and in Latin America. When we feed them we are ministering unto Christ. There are refugees from Cambodia, Vietnam and Laos. When we take them into our communities we are welcoming our Lord among us.

There may be those who see social action purely in terms of political activism and confronting the principalities and powers of this world, but Christian social action must first concern itself with meeting the needs of individuals who have been created in the image of God. C. S. Lewis has written, "If individuals live only seventy years, then a state, or a nation, or a civilization, which may last for a thousand years is more important than an individual. But if Christianity is true, then the individual is not only more important, but incomparably more important, for he is everlasting and the life of a state or a civilization, compared with his, is only a moment."

If we do not try to meet the needs of people near to us and to share the love of Christ with our neighbors, then we have no legitimate right to move on to other types of social action. It is easy to become so concerned with the social injustices that are inherent in our political and economic system that we pass over the suffering of people who confront us face-to-face in daily living. Sometimes we get so caught up in the problems of the world on a societal level that we lose sight of those who may be needy on an individual level. Jesus would remind us that if we cannot respond to those whom we can see, it is impossible to respond to a God whom we cannot see.

THE IDEAS

ADOPT A GRANDPARENT

This service project is great for young people who are mature enough to make a relatively long-term commitment to something. The first step is to take the entire group to visit a convalescent home or the homes of other elderly people who are alone. Allow the kids to mingle with and talk with these people so that they get to know them better.

Afterwards, introduce them to the idea of "adopting" one or more of these seniors as a "grandparent." Each young person would be assigned (or would choose) one or two elderly people to visit on a regular basis, remember on special occasions, take on short trips now and then, and to just be a good friend. This could be planned to continue for a specific amount of time, perhaps a year or maybe even longer.

During the course of the program the young people could share with each other how things are going and what problems they are encountering. The adult youth sponsors could also monitor the program and offer help and encouragement to the kids who are involved. At the end of the term, or at least once a year, the group could sponsor a special banquet or some other gathering in which each young person brings their

"grandparent." Of course, there will be some people who are unable to attend because they are confined to beds or nursing care, but there would be others who could attend. Most young people will find this to be an extremely rewarding experience, and the elderly people involved will appreciate it greatly.

BABYSITTING CO-OP

If your church's educational buildings are vacant during the summer months, look into the possibility of establishing a babysitting co-op staffed by the members of your youth group. Arrange to have babysitting available (by appointment only) for a few hours each day at the church and sign up the young people to sit one day a week or less depending on the size of the group. You'll be surprised at how many grateful parents will leave their youngsters for babysitting while they go shopping or go to meetings, etc. This service can be provided free, or you can accept donations.

The advantage of one central location is that the young people can work there as a team, and have on hand lots of toys, books, and educational materials that they can use with the little children. However, it could be done in people's homes as well. You will probably need to set some guidelines on the ages of children you will be able to accept, and you will need to make sure that there are always enough teens or adults on hand to provide good child supervision.

BANDAGE ROLLING

Bandages are always needed by hospitals overseas in mission fields. By collecting old sheets (clean), kids can cut them into strips (from 2 to 4 inches wide) and roll them into bandages for distribution to missionaries and hospitals. One group held a "Roll-a-thon" and secured sponsors who gave 10 cents to one dollar (or as much as they could) per bandage rolled by the youth group in one day. The group wound up with over 600 bandages.

BIG BROTHERS, BIG SISTERS

Your high school and college young people may want to become "big brothers" or "big sisters" to children in your church or neighborhood who don't have "real" older brothers and sisters. This would simply involve

getting to know them by name and making a point to welcome them each Sunday at church or to pay special attention to them in some other way. It might include visiting them at home on a regular basis, doing special things with them, or picking them up for Sunday School. Perhaps the teens can teach the children a skill or talent such as drawing, playing the guitar, fishing, carpentry, cooking, or any number of things. It's a wonderful way for your youth to be positive role models for younger kids and to contribute a great deal to their development.

BIRTHDAY PARTY FOR JESUS

During the Christmas holidays, it would be a great idea for the youth group to sponsor a "birthday party for Jesus" and invite all the children of the church or neighborhood. It should be planned to include all the usual birthday activities, like games, party hats, streamers, balloons, cake, ice cream, etc. Each child should be instructed to bring a new toy to give to Jesus. Ask parents to make it a toy that will last. Have each child present his or her gift (wrapped) and tell what it is. The gifts can stay wrapped, but the impact is better if the children know what the gifts are.

You can then teach the children that Jesus said, "When you give a gift to one of the least of these (like a poor child in an orphanage), you are giving that gift to me." Since toys are of more value to children than food or clothing (in most cases), they will feel a real sense of having given something special to Jesus on His birthday.

The youth group can plan all the games, provide the refreshments, and take care of the children. The toys that are collected can be given to an orphanage or to an agency that distributes toys to needy children.

BREAD BAKING BASH

Have the kids in your youth group gather up all the ingredients they need to bake up lots of bread — both loaves and rolls. Then have a day of bread baking (a Saturday works best), first preparing the dough, getting it into pans, and then letting it rise. While things are in the oven, the young people can play some games, and just have a good time until the bread is baked.

When the bread is finished, prepare some soup and have a lunch featuring hot soup and freshly-baked bread. (You might have everyone bring a can of soup — any kind — and mix it all together.) After lunch, wrap the other loaves (you should make more bread than the kids can eat) and visit the homes of some elderly people in the church. Spend a short time visiting with them and leave them with a homemade loaf of bread, along with a note of appreciation, like "Thanks for being a part of our church family." They'll love it, and it really helps to build relationships between the young and the old. You could conclude the day with a discussion of what happened while visiting the elderly, and perhaps a Bible lesson relating to "bread."

CHRISTMAS GIFTS FOR THE NEEDY

Here's a project that is always great at Christmas time. It's one of many ways to help young people to think of others who are in need at Christmas, rather than only themselves. It involves the giving of Christmas gifts to families who may not be expecting to receive anything at all because of their economic situations.

Usually the Salvation Army or the local welfare department will be aware of particularly needy families in your area. Try to get some details about them. Get their names, ages, clothing sizes, and so on. Then have the group begin finding gifts that would be appropriate for each family member. People in your church can donate items, but stress that they should be new or in very good condition.

After all the gifts have been collected, have a gift wrapping day at the church and allow the youth to wrap all the presents. Then later that day, you can go Christmas caroling and deliver the gifts to the appropriate families. You might want to have someone dressed up like Santa just for fun. The evening can conclude with fellowship and perhaps a discussion on the project.

CHRISTMAS MISSIONARY DINNER

Have your youth group select some missionaries abroad that the church supports for this special Christmas activity. The group should get to know the missionaries they have chosen by corresponding with them, and also by reading their newsletters. Then begin making plans for a "Missionary Dinner" sometime in November or early December. There should be Christmas decorations and pictures or letters from the missionaries posted so that people can see them. The youth group can cook and serve the meal, which could include some dishes from the country where the missionaries are serving. Adults of the church are invited to the dinner, and following a talent show by the youth and a presentation of the work being done by the missionaries, the people are asked to give a free-will offering. The offering can then be sent to the missionaries as a "Christmas Bonus," which they ordinarily would not get. It is a good idea to hold this event as early as possible (even early November) to make sure the gift of money will be received before Christmas.

CHRISTMAS MITTEN TREE

Here's an idea for the colder climates. At Christmas, have the youth sponsor a "Christmas Mitten Tree" which is designed to collect mittens for children in a nearby orphanage or in one of the poorer sections of the city. A Christmas tree can be placed in the church foyer, and the congregation invited to buy or make a pair of mittens to hang on the tree. People may also bring gifts of food, clothing, or games for boys and girls and place them under the tree. The youth group can then take the mittens and the other gifts to the needy children on Christmas Eve.

CHRISTMAS TREE OF LOVE

Here's a good way to encourage members of your youth group or congregation to cut down on the amount of money that is spent on gifts for each other, and to use that money for giving to missions, relief, and other needs at home and abroad. To help people identify those needs, put up a "Christmas Tree of Love," which can be either a flat cardboard tree (painted green), or a real tree. Hanging on the tree are ornaments which can be removed. Each ornament has a project written on it that needs a specific amount of money or other type of help. The people are asked to take an ornament from the tree and make that their Christmas project. If you use a real tree, you could ask the group to replace each ornament that they take with another as a sign that another need has been met. Make sure that the ornaments represent a wide variety of giving opportunities for people, in both large and small amounts.

CHURCH CAR POOLS

With gas shortages, rising gas prices, and increased air pollution, it makes good sense to car pool whenever possible. Public agencies have tried to get people organized into car pools by setting up special phone numbers, advertising, and so on. Why not try to do something like this for your church functions? You probably have many church members who live close to each other who never ride together, yet have plenty of room in their cars. The youth group can design and promote some sort of system for organizing church car pools and implementing them. Sign-up lists, maps, a special car pool hotline, names of drivers who have room in their cars — any of these things can be tried. Any attempt to cut down on the number of cars on the road will be doing everyone a big favor.

CHURCH PANTRY

Many churches will find it a good idea to maintain a "church pantry" that provides food for needy families. Usually the food is donated and kept in a room at the church. Someone has to take care of it, re-stock it, let people know about it, and so forth. Why not make this a project of the youth group?

The group should plan several food drives each year to keep the pantry full of good nonperishable food items and also on the lookout for families who need assistance. The pastor can work with the youth group to find those people who could benefit from such a project. There are several ideas in this chapter that could be used to collect food for the pantry. An ongoing project like this can be very rewarding for any youth group.

CHURCH VIDEO LIBRARY

By now there are probably a number of people in your church who own videotape cameras and all the equipment that goes with them. If not, then it is probably easy to rent such equipment in your area. Why not make it a youth group project to videotape the services of your church for shut-ins and for those who are ill or out of town? The group can buy the blank video cassettes, tape the services, maintain a library, deliver the equipment to the people who want to view the services, and so on. You may have a few kids in your group who love to mess around with this kind of equipment and such a project would be a very fulfilling challenge to them.

CLOTHING COLLECTIONS

Keep in mind that many people need good second-hand clothing, both at home and abroad. A number of your local rescue missions and other agencies are able to sell used clothing to help meet their operating expenses as well. Yet many Americans continue to discard good clothing simply because styles change slightly. Your youth group can help collect clothing for the needy by using some of the ideas for "Creative Canned Food Drives" also in this chapter. Clothing can be collected the same way as food.

CONVALESCENT HOME MINISTRY

There are hundreds of thousands of elderly people who reside in convalescent hospitals (nursing homes) all over the country. In most cases, they are there because they need regular medical or nursing care. These resident hospitals provide youth groups with a tremendous opportunity for service. It is likely that there are several convalescent homes close to your church or community that would love to have your group involved in some kind of voluntary service.

Every convalescent home has an "activities director" who will gladly give you information and help you plan whatever you choose to do. It would be important for you to begin by contacting either this person or the administrator of the convalescent home to find out whether or not the services of your group will be welcomed. It is extremely unlikely that you will be turned down. Most convalescent homes have a difficult time finding people to come in and do good things for their patients, and they especially enjoy having young people. The activities director will probably be available to come to a meeting of your youth group and prepare your group for visits to the convalescent home, if you so desire. An "orientation" of this type is recommended, and usually the convalescent home is more than willing to provide that service.

Even though convalescent homes take care of people who are losing many of their physical abilities (hearing, walking, sight, etc.), they are basically normal human beings. They are often very old (which is quite normal) but otherwise they are just like everyone else. They enjoy being around other people, they respond to a smile, a touch, kind words, music, laughter, and so on. These are all things that your group can provide for

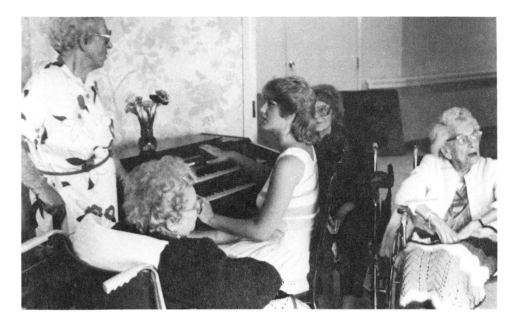

these men and women who often feel isolated from the outside world. Here is a list of things that your youth group can do:

1. Begin some one-on-one visits, perhaps as part of an "Adopt a Grandparent" program. These visits can include conversation, reading to them (sometimes older folks need someone to read their mail to them, or the newspaper, or the Bible, or other books), writing letters for them, or just being a good listener.

2. You can take them on some short trips. Most residents of convalescent homes are permitted to leave the hospital for field trips — to go to a restaurant, a movie, a high school football game, or to church. This can be arranged with the hospital and the patients love it. Some convalescent homes will plan their own outings for the patients, like going to the zoo or to a shopping center, if they have sufficient volunteer help to push the patients around in their wheelchairs. Your group can be a big help in this way. Sometimes all that is needed is someone to push them around the block, or even around the parking lot. They really enjoy getting out of the hospital environment and will be grateful for being able to participate in activities that everyone else takes for granted.

3. You can call them on the phone. Most of the residents of convalescent homes enjoy talking to someone who is interested in them. Once your kids have established a relationship in person, a regular phone calling program can be very significant. It can work both ways — with the kids calling the residents, and the residents knowing that they are free to call their young friends anytime.

4. You can bring programs to the convalescent home. This can include special music, plays, skits, and all sorts of things. You might even consider using the meeting hall at a local nursing home for your regular youth group meeting, and allowing the patients to participate. Another idea is to provide a regular Bible Study for the convalescent home. All this can be set up with the activities director.

5. You can provide music for the patients. If you have any young people who are talented in music, encourage them to share their music with the elderly at a convalescent home. Especially liked are the old hymns and the old songs, but almost anything is appreciated.

6. Play games with them. Most of the patients can play games like Scrabble, Checkers, Dominoes, and so on. There are even some group games that can be played with them, so long as they are not too active.

7. You can provide gifts for them. Like most people, they enjoy receiving gifts of love now and then. A baseball cap to protect their heads when they go outside, a pouch that they can hang on the side of their wheelchair to keep things in, a small bouquet of flowers or a book or tape for them to enjoy can be very appropriate. They also enjoy giving gifts, and they will.

8. You can bring pets or small children to the convalescent home. Most of the residents have almost forgotten what it feels like to hold a small puppy or a kitten, or to touch a small child. Something as ordinary as that can be a major source of joy for an elderly person who is confined to a nursing home.

9. Plant a garden for the patients. There will usually be a small plot of ground near the convalescent home where you can prepare the soil and plant a garden. Let the patients choose what they would like to plant and then they can take care of it to some extent. You will find some people who look forward each day to going out and watering their tomato plant and watching it grow.

There is really no limit to the things that you can do in a convalescent home. Just think creatively and take advantage of this crucial ministry which is right at home. If you aren't aware of any convalescent homes in your area, check the yellow pages of your telephone directory, your local doctor, or contact the American Health Care Association, 1200 Fifteenth Street, N.W., Washington, D.C., 20005 for a listing of local and state nursing home associations.

CREATIVE CANNED FOOD DRIVES

It is always a good idea to collect canned goods (or other nonperishable food items) for distribution to needy families, but here are several creative ways to do it with a youth group and have fun at the same time.

1. Divide the entire group into teams and send them into the neighborhood for a limited time (like one hour) to collect canned goods. The group with the most cans collected inside the time limit wins the prize (or the "honor" of winning). It is amazing how many canned goods your kids can collect when the motivation is a contest of some kind. And for some reason people respond more when they can help someone win a contest.

2. Have a "Scavenger Food Hunt." Give kids a list of nonperishable food items that they need to find and bring back within a given time limit. They can't buy them — they must get them donated by other people. Each item can be worth points according to the difficulty of finding that item. The more of a particular item that they bring back, the more points they get. In other words, the aim is not to just bring back *one* of each item on the list, but as many of each item as possible.

3. At Halloween, have your group go "trick or treating" for canned goods. They can dress up as usual, but at each house they ask the people if they would care to donate one (or more) canned food items to be given to needy families. You can give each family a small thank you note explaining the purpose of the collection and where the food is going. Most people will respond very well to "good goblins" like this.

4. This one could be called a "Way Out Weigh-In." Divide kids into teams (car loads) and have them draw for street names or areas of town. They then have one hour to try to collect as many canned goods or other

nonperishable foods as they can from residents of the area which they drew. The teams report back and weigh-in the food they collected. The team that has the most (by weight) wins a prize of some kind, and all the food is then given to the needy.

5. Here's one the kids will really enjoy. Have the group "kidnap" the pastor or someone else who is well-known in the church (prearranged, of course!) with the ransom being a certain amount of canned goods (e.g., 100 cans) from the congregation to be used for distribution to needy families. This should be done on a Saturday. Kids then telephone people in the congregation informing them of the kidnapping and the ransom. The collection can be made on Sunday morning. If the ransom isn't paid, the youth can be prepared to handle the morning service or the responsibilities of the kidnapped person. To add to the drama, you could mail out "ransom notes" made by cutting letters and words out of magazines. It's a lot of fun and very worthwhile.

6. This one can be given the name "Begging for Benevolence" or something like that. The concept is simple: young people go into the homes of people in the church and "beg" for food for the needy. It should be promoted in advance, with everyone being put on notice that on a certain date the youth group will be coming to people's homes to beg for donatable food items. On the appointed day, the kids head out in pairs with empty boxes, and stop at the homes of as many people as possible, pleading with them to take canned and packaged food items out of their cupboards to fill up the boxes. For effect, the kids can dress up like "beggars" when they pick up the food.

7.   How about a "Supermarket Stake-Out"? Have teams of kids "stake-out" the front doors of large supermarkets, with big boxes that are capable of holding a lot of food. As shoppers enter the supermarket, they are given a slip of paper that simply asks them to purchase one extra item (nonperishable) to be given to the needy. They can deposit that item in the box on their way out. Some people will buy more than one food item, but no one will be obligated to participate if they don't want to. The great thing about this is that people can spend as much or as little as they want. It's up to them. You will, of course, want to clear this with the store manager ahead of time, but usually he will have no objection if you can assure him that the young people will not harrass the customers or create

48

any other problems outside the store. It only means more business and positive publicity for the grocery store. Some stores will even contribute a few food items as well. Pick a good day, and if you have a large youth group, do it simultaneously at several stores in your area.

A CUP OF COOL WATER IN HIS NAME

Here's a service project for those hot summer days. Have the youth group borrow or rent some large coolers (the kind that have a little spout on them) and fill them with fresh water. Then, go to places where there are lots of thirsty people and offer free cups of water. This could be done at the beach, or on a street corner, or in a shopping mall, or anywhere. The cooler could be pulled along in a wagon, a guy could carry it on a backpack frame, or you could set up a table with the cooler and cups on it so that people could just help themselves. A sign on the table or on the cooler could let people know that this is a service of your youth group — in response to the "living water" that Jesus gives.

EASTER BASKETS

A good project for Easter would be to obtain some Easter baskets and fill them with colored eggs and other goodies that could be distributed to underprivileged children. There are children in orphanages, retarded children's homes, hospitals, missions, and poor neighborhoods who never enjoy this aspect of the Easter celebration. Perhaps a group could deliver the baskets and share with the children the story of Easter in word and song.

EASTER CAROLING

Everyone goes caroling at Christmas, so why not at Easter as well? You can go caroling at private homes or you can go caroling at institutions (like convalescent hospitals). If you do go to institutions, be sure to contact them first and let them know what you want to do. It may take a little extra "explaining." Meet an hour or so early to make sure that everyone knows the songs you will be singing. Choose songs of joy that effectively communicate the Easter message. You may want to choose songs that are familiar enough that those being sung to can join in and sing along. Your pastor can come and administer communion to the shut-ins and others if you think it would be appropriate. Another good idea is to get some flowers ahead of time and to present Easter bouquets to those to whom you sing. You will find that because it's so unexpected, caroling at Easter will go over even better than Christmas caroling. Start a new tradition!

EYEGLASS COLLECTIONS

There are many people in third world countries who have problems with their eyesight, but are unable to obtain corrective eyeglasses that will help them to see or read. Your youth group can provide eyeglasses for these people by collecting eyeglasses in your community. People are simply asked to donate their old pairs of eyeglasses, no matter how "out of style" they may be, for distribution to the poor.

Once the eyeglasses are collected, they can be sent to the Evangelical Association for the Promotion of Education (see chapter seven for the address). The glasses are "read" by a lensometer to determine the power or prescription of the lenses. They are labeled and shipped to clinics in the Dominican Republic and Haiti, where the poor are given free eye examinations and, if necessary, an appropriate pair of eyeglasses.

Another agency which distributes eyeglasses to the poor is the Christian Medical Society, Project Eyeglasses, 1820 S.W. 84th St., Miami, Florida 33155.

FREE CAR WASH

This one usually blows everybody's mind. Have your youth group organize a regular car wash (at a gas station, shopping center, or the church parking lot) but instead of selling tickets, have the kids give them away. You may want to make it clear that there are "no strings attached." It really is a "Free Car Wash." You might want to notify the news media ahead of time and ask them to run a story in advance letting people know that this is not just a gimmick, or another way to get people's money. The idea behind the car wash is that it is a free gift from the youth group to the community—a gesture of Christian love and friendship.

You can, of course, accept donations if you want to, but this should not be emphasized if you want to make it a true act of service. You might want to do this on a Saturday and then discuss what happened (the reactions of people, etc.) with your youth group on Sunday.

FRIENDSHIP BOXES

The American Red Cross sponsors a "Friendship Box Program," which involves young people in filling boxes (provided by the Red Cross) with health, educational and recreational items to be distributed to underprivileged children at home and overseas. The youth group buys the material that goes into the boxes — crayons, small toys, toothbrush, puzzles, books, a pad of paper, an attractive card expressing friendship, handmade items, and so on. The boxes are available from the Red Cross for around ten cents each.

If your group works with an orphanage or a children's hospital, etc., then this basic idea could be done on your own so long as you have a good way to distribute the boxes to needy children. For information on the Red Cross program, contact your local chapter.

GARDENS AND GLEANERS

Here are some ideas that will really "grow" on you. They each have to do with vegetable gardens. Everybody loves fresh vegetables, but not everyone is able to plant and tend a garden of their own. So, here are some suggestions:

1. Find some land which is not in use and plant a community garden that can provide food for the elderly, the poor, shut-ins, and so on. Call real estate firms, the city, and look for yourself for a good location. Ask if it could be used for gardening by people who need to supplement their food budgets with fresh vegetables and grains. Then go to seed dealers in the area to see if they will donate packages of garden seeds. Many times they throw away seeds which are about to or have expired. The seeds are usually still potent. When you have secured some land and some seeds, advertise a little bit. Get some free advertising in the local paper or shopping guide. Offer the seeds and the land to the poor of the community. Then have members of your youth group work with these people to develop gardens, pull weeds, water the crops, and so on. After the initial set-up, the project will grow (literally). The people who take advantage of the land and the seeds will gain a sense of independence. They will be eating fresh vegetables, and the kids who help will also benefit from the experience.

2. Along similar lines, you may have some people in your church or community who have some land, but for one reason or another are unable to plant or maintain their own gardens. You could institute an "Adopt-a-Garden" program at your church, in which the youth group "adopts" the gardens of shut-ins, chronically ill, hospitalized or elderly people. The group can supply the seeds, the tools, and the muscle power. They can prepare the soil, plant, cultivate, and ultimately harvest the crops of vegetables, all for the people who own the gardens, and who, of course, are unable to do the work. It makes for some great interaction between the generations when the kids are working with some senior citizens on this.

3. Another adaptation of this is to invite members of your congregation who have gardens of their own to set aside a row or two for giving away to the needy. Again, youth can supply the seeds (if necessary) and after the harvest, deliver the food to people who need it.

4. Lastly, if your community has public garden plots, or is in an area where there are many farms, your group might consider the old custom of "gleaning." Going through the fields after the harvest and salvaging that which is ripe and useable can produce huge amounts of good food for needy people. In most cases it will be necessary to secure permission to do this.

GRAFFITI SQUADS

If you live in the city where there is a lot of offensive graffiti on public walls and on the sides of buildings, volunteer to remove it at no cost to the city or the building owners. You may need to purchase paint or rent the necessary equipment to do the job properly, but a project like this really gets the attention of the community. In fact, it might just bring out a lot of other people who want to join in and help out. Something like this often can develop into a big block party in the middle of the street after all the graffiti has been eliminated, enabling you to get to know some new people and providing an excellent opportunity for Christian witness.

GRANNY'S PLACE

Here's a great way to help the elderly of your community. Find a good location (it could be at your church) and set up a gift shop that is open once a week, or once a month, called GRANNY'S PLACE. Contact all the senior citizens in the church or neighborhood and ask them to make things that can be sold. They can knit, crochet, make a crafts project, a quilt, a woodcarving, or just about anything. The youth group can advertise the store and help work when the store is open. With a little creative effort, this could develop into a very successful business venture. The profits can go back to the elderly people themselves to help supplement their incomes — or they can be used for other mission projects.

H.O.P. CLUB

H.O.P. stands for "Help Older People" and the H.O.P. Club is a program in which teens and adults work together to assist the elderly with work that they are unable to do for themselves. This should be an ongoing ministry as opposed to a one-shot service project type of thing. Skilled adults train the youth to do carpentry, plumbing, wiring, upholstery, or whatever needs to be done, and give direction and supervision while on the job. Younger kids can be involved in such tasks as washing windows and walls, raking leaves, shoveling snow, moving furniture, writing letters, and so on. Many other people who want to be involved, but less directly, can provide financial assistance, etc. The important thing is that it should be well-organized and carried out on a regular basis. Many senior citizens' groups can provide information on where the greatest needs are, and the elderly community can be informed that this service is available at little or no charge to them.

A program such as this not only provides valuable relief for the elderly who normally must pay to have this work done, but also gives kids the opportunity to give of themselves in a meaningful way and to build relationships with a segment of society that they often ignore.

HOSPITAL SPOOK OUT

Here's a service project for Halloween. Take your youth group to the pediatric ward of a hospital on Halloween night all dressed up in costumes (not too scary, though). You will need to call ahead and make the necessary arrangements with the hospital administrators, but they will usually go along with the idea if the group is well-supervised.

Have the group make up in advance some "trick or treat" bags full of goodies to present to each child. The goodies can include things like coloring books, cards, balloons, bubbles, books, and so forth. Some children may be able to have candy, but this should be cleared with the nurses or doctors. The group should visit each child individually and sing "Happy Halloween to you" (to the tune of Happy Birthday) and just have a good time. Make sure the kids are aware of basic hospital etiquette and they will have a very rewarding evening.

HOSPITAL VISITATIONS

There are many people in the hospital who get very few visitors. Get permission through the hospital administrator to bring a few mature young people in on a regular basis to visit some of these people during visiting hours. Nurses on duty can help you know which patients are most willing to have visitors.

It is important that the kids who participate in this be briefed regarding simple hospital etiquette. For example, they should never sit on or lean on the bed; they should always talk softly; if the patient is hard of hearing, they should move closer rather than talk louder; they should be cheerful — they're not at a funeral, etc. Perhaps a professional nurse or your pastor can help the young people know what to do.

The kids should visit patients in pairs. They don't need to take gifts, cards, Bibles, or anything like that. They should just stop in, identify themselves, talk, listen, offer best wishes, and then leave. Sometimes a prayer or Scripture might be appropriate, but only if the patient seems to desire that. The main thing is for the young people to give of themselves to some people who are hurting and often very lonely. It can be a tremendous experience for the kids and a worthwhile ministry as well.

LABOR DAY

The basic idea behind this service project is this: the youth group works for people in the community—doing odd jobs of all kinds—for free. The best way to go about doing this is to first pick a day, like a Saturday or a day when all the kids are out of school. Then get the word out that on this day, the kids will be available to work for anyone who needs them, without pay of any sort.

You could send out a letter to everyone in the neighborhood that reads something like this:

```
Dear Neighbor:

The members of the church youth fellowship want
to show appreciation for our special friends by a
work day. Can we help you in some way? Does your
lawn need mowing? Do you need help getting groc-
eries? Would you want your windows washed? Would
you like us to read to you? Just visit you?

Just mark on the enclosed card how we can be of
some help. If we receive a reply from you, we
will come on  (date)  . Of course, there is no
charge for this. This is a gift of love.

                              Sincerely yours,
```

Another way to do this would be to distribute flyers around the community announcing that on a given day the youth group will be passing by in the church bus looking for work to do. If anyone would like some help, they should simply tie a handkerchief onto the doorknob of their front door. Then, the group just cruises up and down streets looking for houses that have handkerchiefs tied to the front doorknob.

There are many different ways to do this. It can be a one-shot kind of thing, or it could develop into an ongoing project that involves the kids in a "labor day" once a month or more. You can make it open to anybody who needs work done, or you can limit it to elderly people, those who are handicapped, or people from a certain socio-economic class. That is up to you.

One criticism that could be leveled at your group as a result of this (or perhaps any other service project as well) is: "Sure, they will work hard for other people, but they won't do any work at home." The point may be well-taken, so you may want to help kids to understand that demonstrating the love of Christ needs to begin at home. By doing their chores without having to be reminded over and over, or by cleaning their room before they head out on another service project, they can expect to get a lot more positive support from parents.

MIGRANT MINISTRY

In rural communities there is a great need for ministry among migrant farm workers. These are people who have left their homes for seasonal work, and in most cases they are living in migrant labor camps. You can get information regarding migrant workers in your area by contacting local farmers or the local farm labor bureau. Many of these people have their entire families with them, so you might want to begin by meeting the young people of the migrant camp and planning some activities with them. You can take them to movies, plan social events or do other fun things with these kids whose lives are often drab and uneventful.

If there aren't any children or youth involved, the group can still have a ministry to the workers themselves. One possibility would be to rent or otherwise obtain a good film in the workers' native language (if they don't speak English) and take the church movie projector out to the camp and show the film for them. Refreshments can be served and the youth in your group can get to know these people a little bit and perhaps be sensitized to their needs and life style.

Another possibility is to take the church bus out to the migrant camps on Sunday and bring as many of these workers to church as would like to attend. Let them know that they don't have to dress up. You might want to provide an interpreter during the service if necessary. Afterwards, have a church potluck supper that includes them. You'll find that your church can have a tremendous ministry to these people in many different ways.

MILITARY MINISTRY

If your church is located anywhere near a military base, then you have quite a few young men and women in the area who are away from home and who are probably very lonely most of the time. Contact the base chaplain or other officers who can help make contact with these people. Many times it is possible to bring programs onto the military base itself, or the service people can simply be invited to participate in your youth group or church activities. Perhaps a periodic social event would be appropriate, designed especially to help these people make some new friends. Men and women who are in the service will appreciate the opportunity to have some civilian contacts and to be treated like normal human beings. They need the church now more than ever, just as the church needs them.

MINISTRY TO THE RETARDED

In every city there are institutions which care for people who are "developmentally handicapped" or mentally retarded. In most cases, they are understaffed and operate on a shoestring budget. They can use all the help they can get. If there is a mental institution or retarded children's home in your area, it can provide a wide variety of opportunities for your young people to minister to some special human beings who, like themselves, have been created in the image and likeness of God.

Preparation is always important when doing service projects, but especially so with a ministry to the retarded. Young people who are totally unprepared may become frightened or upset at the actions or conditions of those who are retarded. It might be a good idea to start with a visit to the institution rather than to try and "do something" right away. Usually a staff person from the institution can help the group with their questions

and concerns.

Here are a few things that any group can do with retarded persons who are residents of institutions:

1. Bring music to them. Retarded people love music with an intensity that can be surprising. A few young people with guitars or other instruments will go over big.

2. Play games with them. Frisbee throwing, ball games, active games of all kinds are great.

3. Bring some arts and crafts projects and work on them together.

4. Talk to them. Develop a friendship with one person. Help that person with letter writing and other simple tasks that may be difficult. Go on walks with that person and take him or her places. In most cases, retarded people are allowed to leave the institution so long as some responsible person is with them.

5. Provide a church service at the institution. Include a lot of singing and Bible stories.

6. Participate in a "Special Olympics." This nationally-known event is conducted in local communities all over the country, and most institutions need volunteers who will be coaches, helpers, and escorts.

7. Bring a few retarded young people to your youth group meetings. You will find that they will contribute a great deal to the quality of your group.

NEWSPAPER WATCH

Appoint a committee in your youth group to watch the local newspaper during the week for people who have experienced tragedies or who have special needs that the group might be able to meet. Maybe some family's home was destroyed in a fire and they need clothes or lodging; or perhaps someone was seriously injured in an accident and he or she needs help with housework, or just needs to be visited. The best way to determine what to do would be to list the items chosen from the paper and then ask, "What can we do?" for each one. Then narrow it down to the one or two that your group would be able to do best and go to it. This helps kids to develop a sensitivity to the "news," and makes them aware that real people and real lives are affected by what they hear and read in the media.

PARTY TIME

A party doesn't sound like a service project, but it can be. Sometimes the best way to show someone that you really care about them is to throw a party in their honor.

So, how about putting on a gala party for all the senior citizens in your church? Plan some games that they would enjoy, come up with some fun entertainment, sing songs that they know, serve refreshments, and just have a great time. Send special invitations well in advance letting the seniors know that this is the youth group's way of honoring them in a special way. The response will probably be very positive.

The same can be done for children or others who may not have the resources or the energy to plan great parties. It's an excellent way to express Christian love and to get to know other people better.

PRISON MINISTRY

In every city there are jails, prisons, juvenile halls, reform schools, detention camps, and correctional institutions of all kinds. One of the specific instructions Jesus gave the church was to minister to the needs of prisoners. It would not be an overstatement to say that to neglect this ministry would be an act of disobedience on the part of the church. Today most of our jails and prisons are filled to capacity with human beings who have been written off as "the least of these." The following ideas, suggested by Chuck Workman of Bravo Ministries in San Diego, are just a few of the ways that your youth group or your entire church might become involved in a ministry to prisoners. If you would like more information about prison ministry, a good contact would be Prison Fellowship (see Chapter Seven).

1. *Church Services:* The best way for a church or youth group to become involved is to provide a good church service within an institution. The U.S. Constitution guarantees individuals the freedom of worship and institutions are therefore obligated to allow their residents this privilege. It is important to understand that this does not grant a church the right to come in and use manipulation, intimidation, or the imposition of guilt, fear and shame to bring the wicked to repentance. An effective church service should instead focus itself on the needs of the inmates without violating the rules of the institution and common decency. Special music,

movies, guest speakers, etc., can all be employed along with traditional singing and preaching to bring to the men and women a message of hope and salvation. Far too often the church is looked upon as irrelevant by both staff and inmates. Good planning and a sense of responsibility and caring can prevent this.

2. *Book Drives:* Many librariers within institutions are in terrible shape. The selection is usually poor and the condition of the books leave much to be desired. Churches have often been very good about providing Bibles and religious reading material, but these often pile up in storerooms and are ignored. A youth group could offer a tremendous service to an institution by providing books for its library. The institution may have a list of books that are needed, or the youth group could put together its own list. There are many good books by the world's greatest authors that could be procured. Also, "how-to" books on languages, typing, bookkeeping, law, philosophy, ethics, history, and many others would be excellent. A practical gift like this would make a profound impact on both staff and residents alike and do much to improve the church's image.

3. *Special Music:* The church has been faithful in providing good music of the religious variety, but institutions are often starved for music that is just for entertainment. Music is a powerful force for everyone, but even more so to an inmate. It is often his only communication with the outside world and maybe his only means of emotional escape. A church or youth group could provide some regular entertainment that would not compromise the principles of the church.

4. *Big Brother/Big Sister Programs:* It is often possible to pair up an inmate with a person from the community in a "Big Brother" or "Big Sister" type of ministry. Some programs along these lines are already established, but the church may want to create its own program. Loneliness within an institution can be crippling, and the presence of a "friend" can make all the difference to an inmate's adjustment. It can also be a strong link to survival when the inmate is released to have concerned individuals and a strong church offering some support.

5. *Pen Pals:* For those in churches who cannot or do not wish to be involved personally with the inmates, letter-writing can be a very good ministry. Inmates are avid writers. Many will write so often that postage becomes a problem. To receive a letter during mail-call brightens up one's day. Many churches do not have a correctional institution close by, and this is one way they can reach behind the walls and touch someone's life. This is also great for young people who may not be allowed in prisons because they are under age.

6. *Guest Speakers:* Institutions are not very intellectually stimulating, and churches could perform a real service by providing good speakers once in a while. There are some excellent speakers (not preachers) who would be very well-received in a prison, such as public figures, politicians, sports figures, people from the entertainment industry, educators, former offenders, attorneys, etc.

7. *Sports:* Most institutions have some type of intramural sports program. The problem with this is that they are playing each other over and over and it gets boring after a while. Churches usually are welcome to bring in a group to play against an institutional team. You can play basketball, softball, volleyball, horseshoes, chess, checkers, or almost any game. The advantage to this is that it makes all the players equal, breeds much laughter, and makes the residents feel part of society again.

8. *Special Services:* Churches are storehouses of talent, and institutions are often bereft of talent. Churches can offer their talent to the institution for the benefit of the inmates. Medical doctors can volunteer their services as well as attorneys, psychologists, dentists, teachers, social workers, etc. Tradesmen can offer their skills in carpentry, electrical, plumbing, etc. Women can become an invaluable source by cooking and sewing for those who can't. Virtually any talent an individual has can be employed to help those in need.

9. *Special Gifts:* Even in good years, when the economy is booming, most institutions don't have much money to work with. Churches could ask what items were most needed by an institution and buy them — for example, a new sound system, new chairs, curtains or sports equipment. If there is no one item the church wants to purchase they might consider a cash gift to be used at the institution's discretion.

10. *Political Activities:* Correctional institutions are caught in a tough position today. Society wants its offenders locked away for longer periods of time, yet refuses to vote in funds for the construction of more or better prisons. Thus, more and more people are forced into institutions where the quality of life (which never was good) quickly deteriorates. The church can do much to become knowledgeable and active in the field of correctional reform. This one area, more than any other, could build the credibility of the church among the institutional population. Lobbying, letter-writing, rallies, speaking, books, etc., could be employed to help alleviate incredibly bad living conditions and ease the suffering of many hurting people.

All of these ideas are worth checking into. Some are more appropriate for youth groups than others. If you need more information on what is possible in your area, contact your local government, talk to officials who work withinn the institutions — like the prison chaplain (if there is one) — and they will try to help you decide upon a project that would be appropriate for your group.

PUPPET MINISTRY

Here's one that is very popular with a lot of youth groups. The idea is to develop a good puppet program, complete with a wide selection of "Muppet" style puppets, scenery, props, and so on. There are several companies that produce puppets, scripts, recorded programs, sound equipment, and the like. There are also seminars available that instruct kids on how to put on very professional puppet shows.

Once your group has both puppets and a program, take it out to underprivileged areas where there are a lot of children. This could be an inner-city area, an Indian reservation, an orphanage or children's hopsital, or any number of places. The aim is to bring a fun, entertaining program with a message to kids who rarely get to experience that sort of thing. You will find that many of your young people will get very excited about this kind of ministry.

RAKE AND RUN

This is a service project that kids really enjoy and which goes over great with the whole neighborhood. On a given day, all the members of the youth group gather for a day of raking leaves. They should all bring their own leaf rakes. Then, you load everybody up on the church bus, or in the back of a truck, and cruise up and down streets looking for houses that obviously need to have leaves raked. One member of the group goes up to the door of the house, knocks, and finds out whether or not the people desire to have their leaves raked. If the answer is yes, all the kids pile out of the bus and rake the lawn. With fifteen or twenty kids, it will only take five minutes to rake the leaves and bag them. Let people know that this is being done for free.

Kids should be reminded that they are on other people's property and that they should be careful not to damage anything by carelessness or horsing around. When the job is finished at each house, the kids can leave a "calling card" from the youth group that offers best wishes and lets the people know who they are. Most people are very impressed and the kids really feel good about what they have done.

During the winter, this event can be called "Snow and Blow" (shoveling snow off people's sidewalks). During the spring, you could call it "Splash and Split" (washing people's windows), or "Mow and Blow" (mowing people's lawns). In each case the idea is to give an unexpected act of kindness to others.

RECYCLE A WRECK

If you have any mechanics or mechanically-inclined boys (or girls) in your youth group, you might try this idea. Pick up an old car that doesn't run very well or which needs a new engine, and fix it up for a family who can't afford to buy one of their own. You can usually buy used cars that are in pretty bad shape for almost nothing. The youth group can then fix the car up for a reasonable amount—using rebuilt engine parts, used (but good) tires, etc. This would provide someone with some good, cheap transportation. It would probably be a good idea to have some adult supervision. This might also be a good way for some kids to learn a skill.

REFUGEE MINISTRY

You may live in an area where there is a steady influx of refugees. Most heavily populated areas in the United States (especially cities like Los Angeles and New York) have many refugees and refugee families seeking shelter, food and clothing. The following ideas have been provided by World Relief (see Chapter Seven), and they offer a variety of ways for young people to become involved with refugees in this country. For more information on refugees, contact your local World Relief office.

1. Take responsibility for one part of a World Relief "Refugee Sponsoring Committee." You can arrange for food to be supplied, collect clothing, locate and help to collect furniture, or arrange for transportation to offices, meetings, shopping, etc.
2. Help set up refugees' apartments (paint, clean, arrange furniture.
3. Help obtain furniture and clothing for them (possibly by taking the refugees to garage sales and flea markets).
4. Help teach the refugees English-as-a-Second-Language (ESL).
5. Babysit while parents attend ESL or job training classes.
6. Teach refugees how to use public transportation.
7. Involve them in American sports (if they are interested) by taking them to games, or teaching them to play.
8. Take them on field trips to zoos, the circus, museums, plays, etc.
9. Have a book drive to obtain children's books, Bibles, and others for the families.
10. Hold classes for the families—cooking, handicrafts, or music.

11. Organize and take classes taught by the refugees on their cooking, handicrafts, language, etc. Refugees receive so much, they need the opportunity to give, too!
12. Plan socials involving the young people — let them include some ideas from their culture — food, games, whatever.
13. Help tutor the young people in school subjects.
14. Assist them in filing for Social Security, Permanent Residence, or U.S. Citizenship.
15. Volunteer time to a local World Relief office — for filing, typing, mailing — the offices will be able to share their needs.

You or your group will probably have many more ideas for ways to help. If you can raise money for the refugees in your area, there are many ways it can be used, e.g., for Bibles, baby furniture, etc. The most important thing that anyone can do for the refugees is to offer friendship. Besides helping them in a difficult time of transition, you can enrich your own life by learning and sharing with the refugee friends you make.

RUNAWAY HOMES

There is a great need for temporary emergency shelter for runaway young people across the country. Your youth group can help provide such shelter. Check with local authorities to find out whether or not there is a problem with runaways in your area. Chances are there will be if you live near a city. You might want to have someone from your local youth services bureau, juvenile court system, or police department come and talk to the youth group about the problem.

Once you have determined the need, have the kids in your youth group, with adult supervision, select and interview families in the church and the community for the purpose of recruiting "host homes." Those families that are chosen will also need to be briefed by the local department of youth services, or whichever agency handles the relocation of runaway youth. These "host homes" are then put on call to house a runaway young person for a temporary period of time.

You will need to check with local authorities to determine how long a youth may stay in a temporary shelter. A local attorney can easily help the group compose simple "release papers" including a parental consent form for the parents of the runaway to sign, permitting their child to reside in a host family location. This information is always kept confidential.

The principle role of the youth group is to recruit and maintain host families for the program, as well as to welcome the runaway young people into the youth group activities. The juvenile courts and other authorities can handle the rest.

SENIOR SURPRISE

This is a service project which will help bridge any generation gap. Find out the birthdates of the senior citizens in your congregation. Assign these dates to different members of your group who will be responsible for baking a cake on that day. Besides a cake, you will need to furnish the following: paper plates, plastic forks, a knife, napkins, candles, milk (you can't eat cake without milk), ice cream, a small cooler for the ice cream, a card (this could be made by someone in the group), and even a present if there is someone that is good at making things like pillows, plaques, etc.

On the senior's birthday, go to his or her house without notice and have everyone sing "Happy Birthday." Then, invite yourself in and tell the person that he or she is "guest of honor" and that you are throwing a party for them. Proceed to cut, serve, and pass out the food, and have a good time, not neglecting to clean up any mess that is made.

If you really want to surprise the senior citizens in your church, have a senior surprise party for them to celebrate the day of their baptism. They'll really feel good to know they are younger than they thought (and it won't take as many candles!). Either way, this is an excellent way to get to know the elderly people of your church or community. They will feel loved and you'll be "surprised" at how good you feel by doing it.

SERVANT WEEK

This is a summer activity that could be done in addition to or in place of a normal summer camp. It requires a full week, and it could be done like a "lock-in" where the kids camp out for a week inside the church. The emphasis of the week is "servanthood," with the first part of the week (a day or so) spent doing some Bible study on the subject. Kids need to know how important the concept of serving others is to the Christian life.

The rest of the week is spent actually doing service projects. One day can be spent working around the church, another can be spent visiting or working in a convalescent home, another day can be spent putting on a children's program, etc. Each day should be different with a different emphasis. This book should give you a lot of good ideas. The kids can discuss the experiences of each day in the evening back at the camp.

Something like this will take a lot of advance preparation, but the rewards are great. You will find that your young people will have their lives affected much more profoundly by a week of serving others than by going away for a week of fun and inspiration at summer camp.

SPONSOR A CHILD

There are many agencies like World Vision and Holt International (see Chapter Seven) which try to find financial sponsors for children in orphanages overseas. Usually these agencies will ask for a certain amount of money to provide food, clothing and shelter for particular children each month. Most of the time you can select a child to sponsor by name and receive detailed information about the child, including photos, and sometimes handwritten thank-you notes from the child.

Why not ask your church group to "adopt" one of these children and pledge to support the child on a monthly basis? Each person in the youth group can give a certain amount, like $1.00 per month, and the child's progress can be monitored by the entire group. The group will know the child's name and will really feel involved in that child's life. The group can also pray for the child on a regular basis. Not only is a project like this easy to do, it helps young people to develop a world awareness and a sense of compassion for others.

STAY-AT-HOME WORK CAMP

Most work camps are done at a far away location — like Mexico, an Indian reservation, or an Appalachian village — but they don't have to be. You can have a work camp right at home.

Find a place in or out of town where your group can sleep and eat during the whole period of the work camp (four to seven days). The kids do need to be away from their homes during the work camp, if possible. Then, find projects nearby that need to be done. These can include painting, remodeling, fixing roofs, clean-up work, weeding, and all sorts of jobs for people who can't afford to have it done themselves. Many of the same guidelines and suggestions in chapter four of this book would be applicable to a "Stay-At-Home Work Camp."

The only real disadvantage of this (compared to a work camp that is far away) is that there may be unwanted distractions. This is something you would have to deal with. But the advantages are many. You will be able to accomplish more with less expense, you will probably be able to involve more kids, and you will be able to have an impact on your immediate community. It is also much easier to plan and to do follow-up work. Of course the important thing is not whether you do a work camp at home or abroad. The main thing is just to do one. The results will always be worth the effort.

STUDY WAR NO MORE

Christian young people are becoming increasingly aware and concerned about world peace and the prevention of nuclear war. Most young people, however, feel unable to do anything significant to lessen the danger of war and nuclear holocaust. Yet there are some positive things that a youth group can do.

For example, the group can sponsor a series of programs featuring Bible study on peacemaking, films and lectures on the dangers of nuclear war, and workshops to decide on possible action. The group can plan a worship service of peace, make banners and posters, write letters, march in peace rallies, and do many other things to promote peace and to discourage war. Chapter five of this book offers some good suggestions on how to effect political change and to influence those who are in power.

An excellent resource containing ideas for groups is a booklet entitled *Peace Is Possible* by Shirley J. Heckman (United Church Press, 132 West Thirty-first Street, New York, NY 10001). There are many other books and resources currently being published that would also be helpful in planning a series of meetings or deciding upon possible action to take. Agencies like Catholic Relief Services and the Mennonite Central Committee (see Chapter Seven) also provide resources for Christian groups.

SUMMER JAMBOREE

Have your high school or college-age youth conduct a Vacation Bible School during the summer for an inner-city neighborhood. There are usually hundreds of children in these areas who have nothing to do except to play in the streets. A "V.B.S." can be done in cooperation with an inner-city church that hasn't the staff to put one on themselves, or you can simply rent a community hall, use a public park or some other location. You might call it Summer Jamboree, or any other name you choose.

The best way to prepare for this would be to involve your young people in a normal Vacation Bible School at your own church. Usually high schoolers aren't too excited about V.B.S., but if they know that they are going to be putting one on themselves the following week they will take an active role in the first one just to learn.

Advertise your Summer Jamboree throughout the neighborhood. The program itself can consist of the usual things — games, Bible stories, puppets, crafts, singing, refreshments, and so on. It can last one or two weeks, mornings or afternoons. Have one day when you invite the parents to come see the activities and a program put on by the kids. Several churches have done this and the results have been tremendous.

THANK YOU, OFFICER

Believe it or not, most police officers and others in law enforcement are NOT brutal, tough, impersonal, or corrupt. In fact, the majority of them are average people who have families and friends and who have chosen a profession that puts their lives in great danger while helping others. Rarely do they receive thanks from the public. Mostly they get bad press.

So, why not suggest to your youth group that they do something nice for the cops in town. Maybe you can have a lock-in at the church that begins around 6:00 p.m. Spend the first few hours making a big banner that says something like, "Thanks for a job well-done!" Make some cookies, brownies, cupcakes, etc., and then hit the police station around midnight (when they usually change shifts). This should be prearranged with the police department, of course. Put up the banner and pass out the goodies to all the officers who are either coming or going. You'll find that many of them will be genuinely moved by this and will want to stay and talk to your young people for a long time. It's a great way to share the love of Christ with people who don't see very much of it on the job. This can also be done for firemen and other public employees.

TOY COLLECTION

Most cities and towns have organizations which collect toys at Christmas for needy children. A good group activity would be to have a toy drive with your young people going door-to-door to collect old unwanted toys that are usable, or that require minor repairs. If necessary, they can be repaired and given to the proper agency for distribution. Check the ideas under "Creative Canned Food Drives" for some good ways to collect toys, too.

TRASH BASH

Collecting trash from streets and vacant lots is a community service project that goes over great with everybody. A "Trash Bash" is one good way to organize and promote this with your youth group. The best approach is to divide your group into teams of five or six each and to assign them to different areas of the community. Each person should carry a heavy duty trash bag and wear gloves. As each bag of trash is collected, it can be tied and placed in large dumpsters provided by a trash collection company.

One group has turned this into a "marathon" event, with kids

working around the clock (taking turns) to establish a record of 200 consecutive hours of trash collecting. Usually something like this attracts the attention of the local news media and the city officials who give the group a lot of encouragement and praise.

TUTORING MINISTRY

There are many children who need tutoring in basic subjects like arithmetic and reading. Without such tutoring, they have extreme difficulty with the subject and begin to feel like failures. In addition, there are children who have minor learning disabilities which can be overcome with some tutoring and some positive reinforcement.

You may have several young people in your youth group who would be well-qualified to tutor a child in a given subject. Usually this means getting together with the child each day, or every other day, to work on homework and to offer some patient instruction in the subject. Perhaps your group would see this as a ministry and offer themselves as tutors for free. Some parents, however, may want to pay something for the service. Either way, it can be a tremendous opportunity for a young person to contribute to the education and development of a child. It's also good experience for youth who may want to enter the teaching profession. It would probably be a good idea to seek some professional help (teachers, professional tutors, etc.) to give your youth some training and guidance in the fundamentals of tutoring.

WELCOMING THE HANDICAPPED

Your youth group can have a significant ministry to young people who are physically handicapped. In all likelihood, there are hundreds of teen-agers and young adults in your area who are confined to wheelchairs, vision or hearing-impaired, or seriously handicapped in some other way. Few of them will be involved in a regular church youth program because most youth groups are unable to make them feel welcome.

Why not encourage your group to follow the example of Jesus and make friends with some handicapped young people? You might begin by bringing in some professionals (doctors, nurses, social workers, etc.) who can help educate the group as to the special needs and problems of the handicapped. Let the kids ask questions and work through any hang-ups that they might have concerning handicapped people.

Then invite some handicapped young people to come to your youth group meetings. Provide transportation if necessary. If it is appropriate, ask them to talk about their particular handicap and to share some of their feelings with the group. Allow the other members of the group the opportunity to get to know them. Try to plan your meetings in such a way that everyone, whether handicapped or not, can be included.

You may want to work with local hospitals or other agencies (like schools that provide special education for the handicapped). They can help you contact handicapped young people who might want to become a part of a Christian youth group. Once they are there, conduct your meetings in a normal fashion — but inclusive of everyone. In most cases you can even continue to play games and do active things that you always do, so long as you provide your handicapped kids with a way to feel a part. One youth group made a handicapped boy who was confined to a wheelchair their "official youth group photographer." When the rest of the kids were playing games and running around, the handicapped boy was busy taking pictures with an instant camera. After the games were over, the kids would gather around him to look at all the pictures.

Any youth group can be a place where the physically handicapped are welcomed. If you and your youth group are willing to make a few adjustments, the opportunities for ministry are enormous. Of course, it works both ways: your handicapped young people will have a real ministry to the group as a whole. Their presence will make a positive difference.

WINDSHIELD WITNESSING

Find a parking lot with a lot of cars in it and supply the youth group with window cleaning materials (soap, rags, squeegees,etc.). The kids move up and down rows in twos and clean dirty windshields on cars, leaving a note similar to this:

```
Dear Shopper:
    Your windshield was cleaned while you were
shopping by the youth group of First Community
Church. Of course, there is no charge for this.
We just wanted to make your day today a little
brighter. We also hope you'll "see your way
clear" to attend the church of your choice this
week. God bless you!
```

Some people may want to make a donation to the youth group, but make sure the kids do this strictly for free. Also, make sure kids are careful not to climb all over cars, or to scratch somebody's expensive paint job. You might prefer setting up a "window washing station" where people bring their cars, rather than just doing them without permission. Most people will really appreciate having their windows cleaned, but you might find some who don't want anyone touching their car. Use your own judgment here.

WISDOM GATHERING

Have members of your youth group visit senior citizens in your church or community and get to know them better. Take a cassette tape recorder along and ask them a few questions about life that might be helpful to the rest of the youth group. For example, ask them to share their thoughts on marriage, love, friendship, commitment, death, hardship, patience, work, or whatever subject you are interested in. Most seniors think that today's youth don't want to listen to the advice of past generations, but if given the chance, they will offer some sincere words of wisdom. Edit the tapes and bring them back to your next youth group meeting for discussion. Your senior adults can be one of your best program resources.

YOUNG AND WISE BANQUET

Here's a great way to bring your young people and the senior citizens of your church and community together. Have your youth group plan a banquet, complete with a program, and invite senior citizens to come as their guests. The youth can either pay for the food (catered), bring it potluck-style, or prepare it themselves. However, it is usually best that the kids not have to spend too much time with meal preparation, as they need to have time to spend with their invited guests. Each kid is assigned certain senior citizens to pick up, take home, and sit with during the banquet. Invitations are sent to the senior citizens along with R.S.V.P. forms that they can send back. If you are sure to plan a menu that senior citizens can eat, keep the program brief and lively, make plans quite a few weeks in advance, and promote it well, you'll be assured of a successful evening. One church has done this two years in a row with more than 175 senior citizens attending each year.

YOUTH EMPLOYMENT DAY

Do some research during the latter part of the spring to find out what summer job opportunities there might be for the youth of your community. Find out from employment agencies (and anywhere else you can think of) what jobs are going to be available. Then announce in the high school, or wherever the kids hang out, that there will be a Youth Employment Day at your church on a given Saturday. You will want to have as many employers as possible there on that day to do interviews and to take job applications. You will, of course, need to do a lot of preliminary work on this in order to get the cooperation of all those companies and agencies that are doing any hiring. Often your local employment agencies will cooperate in such a program without a charge.

You might also want to conduct some workshops the first part of the day on "How to handle a job interview," or "How to find the job you want." This can be a real service to kids who don't have a clue as to how they are going to spend their summer months. It's a great way for the church to show the youth of the community that they really care about them.

YOUTH GROUP LIMO SERVICE

There are no doubt elderly people in your church who never get to attend certain functions or events because they don't have transportation, and they can't afford to call a taxi. So why not organize some kind of "Limo Service" that provides, free of charge, transportation for these people. You will need to find out who your good drivers are, and then find out when they would be available for such a service. The gas could be paid for from the youth group treasury.

Chapter Four

Workcamps and Mission Trips

by Bill McNabb

The purpose of this chapter is to explore the subject of extended service projects, specifically the workcamp, and to offer some practical advice on how to plan and execute such a project. A workcamp is a planned and guided experience of Christian community in which a group of volunteers, under the sponsorship of a local church or other agency, involves itself in a short-term service project to persons or groups beyond the local church.

Workcamps can take many forms. The volunteer participants may be junior or senior high youth, young adults or older adults. The experience may last from a few days to an entire summer. The variety of possible projects is almost endless.

You can: Work on an orphanage or school,
Repair a run-down church,
Conduct a VBS or Day-Care project,
Assist the elderly in home maintenance,
Participate in urban housing renewal,
Work on a camp or retreat center,
Set up food distribution programs.

All of these options and many more are open to groups which will open their eyes to the needs of others and are willing to extend themselves in service.

Why Do a Workcamp?

There are many reasons to do a workcamp or extended service project — any one of which would be sufficient rationale for the considerable time and energy it takes to do such a project. Here are four of the more cogent ones.

First, there is the scriptural mandate. As Tony Campolo noted in Chapter One, service is a necessary and integral part of the Christian life. You can serve and not be a follower of Christ, but you can't be a follower of Christ and not serve. The Bible tells us that we are to be the hands and feet of Jesus, continuing His work of compassion to the needy.

Second, there is the educational impact of service. So often in the church, education consists of two things: talking and reading. Yet educational psychologists have known for years that these are two of the *least* effective ways of teaching people. The best learning will result from "direct personal experiences" which provide opportunities for discovery and reflection.

A workcamp can be a powerful life-altering experience which can teach in one week more about mission and service than a lifetime of Bible studies or Sunday school classes. In my years of leading workcamps in Mexico and Jamaica, I have seen young people's perceptions of themselves and their purpose in life radically changed by a workcamp experience. There is nothing that makes one appreciate his lot in life more than living with those in poverty for a while. The most common statement I get from parents when their son or daughter returns from such an experience is, "What did you do to my kid?!" There is an appreciation and gratitude that invariably accompanies such a week. It is almost always true that the work a group does is secondary in importance to what happens to the individuals who are doing the work. The paint put upon a building will soon peel off, the ditch that is dug will soon fill up, the building that is built will eventually fall into decay, but a life brought into the power of the mission of Christ and given a sense of direction will never be the same.

Third, the process of preparing for a workcamp, as well as the actual work experience, develops a powerful sense of community in a group. It often seems that when the focus of a group is building community, the goal is eluded. But when the focus is shifted from the group itself to service to others, a profound sense of community comes as a by-product of that service. There is no way that people can travel together, work together side by side, relax together and not draw closer to each other.

Workcamp experiences can also equip young people for leadership roles in the youth group and the church at large. A comment often heard by youth leaders following a workcamp experience is, "The youth who went on the workcamp evolved into the strong leaders of our group. They seem to have a better grasp of what the church is all about."

Fourth, a workcamp does provide genuine and vital aid to people who are in great need. In spite of what was said earlier about the primary benefits being for the volunteers, there are also tremendous benefits for the recipients of a work project. There are many orphanages, church camps, inner-city projects and small churches that would be hard pressed to continue their ministry without the help of workcamp volunteers. I have been involved with orphanages in Tijuana, Mexico, that were built over the years entirely by volunteer workcamp labor and which depend on such labor for continued maintenance. Good workcamps do not consist of "make-work" projects, but are designed to meet a real and specific need. It must always be kept in mind that although the participants benefit greatly, the ultimate goal of the work project is to show God's love through ministry and service to others. It is in giving to others that we add new dimensions to our own lives.

Planning a Workcamp

The first and the most difficult task in planning a workcamp is finding a suitable project. If the work is not meaningful and plentiful, or if it does not fit the nature of the group, it can doom the trip from the very beginning. Here are some items to consider when looking at possible projects.

First, consider the distance. How far can you travel and what will your mode of transportation be? How much time do you have for the trip? Most workcamps shoot for four or five days of work plus travel time.

Second, consider the setting. Do you want a rural setting like a retreat ground or camp or an urban experience at an inner-city church or urban mission project? How about a college or an orphanage?

Third, consider the type of work that your group would like to do. What are the skills and abilities of your members and leaders? You may choose to do manual labor or a project with more direct personal contact such as a tutoring program or conducting a vacation church school program. Perhaps the best approach would be to remain open to any kind of work as long as it is meaningful and is meeting a real need.

You can begin worksite selection by writing to your denominational mission headquarters. Most denominations have either national or regional offices which will match volunteering groups with receiving groups. There are also numerous independent mission and service agencies that can assist in locating good projects. (See Chapter Seven for a list of agencies.)

Write to the project sites which seem best-suited to the needs of your group. Keep in mind that due to a variety of factors, many responses will be negative. That is why it is best to send out several requests, realizing that you may not get the project that was your first choice. When writing, provide information on the number of people that you anticipate taking, the dates you will be available, and the kind of experience you are looking for. Ask about the type of work that needs to be done, the housing and feeding options available, and any costs your group will have to pay. In later letters ask about equipment needed for work, suitable clothing for the climate, and any policies the receiving group might have concerning workcamp groups.

Leadership for the workcamp must be selected and recruited with careful consideration of the nature of the work and the group. Avoid the temptation to either rush out and ask whomever seems available or to accept the offer of some well-meaning but otherwise unacceptable person. Some factors to consider in selecting leaders are: Does the person have the personal relationship skills to get along with young people? Do they have any work skills that would be useful on the trip? Is the person flexible and open to the inevitable fluctuations that occur in any workcamp? Do they have good health and enough energy to keep up with a rigorous schedule?

You may want to draw up a list of qualifications which you feel a good adult leader should have. Think of persons who might fulfill these qualifications and then go after them. After asking them to give up a week of vacation or time away from their families, it is not appropriate to ask them to also pay their own way. The costs for adult leaders should be figured into the initial budget of the trip. Be sure to recruit and get commitments as early as possible since many adults will have to apply months in advance for vacation time. An early start will increase your chances of getting the leaders you want.

Speaking of finances, one of the first questions which comes up when a workcamp is proposed is: "How are we going to pay for the trip?" There are basically three approaches:

1. Have the participants conduct fund-raising projects. the proceeds of which pay the total cost.
2. Receive contributions or subsidies from sources such as the church budget or individuals.

3. Divide the total cost of the trip by the number of participants and have each person pay that amount.

It is probably best to use combinations of the above approaches. For example, the church mission budget could pay for the adult leaders, the group could do a few fund-raisers to lower the cost of the trip, and the participants could pay the remainder themselves. It is best that the workcampers not be "given" the trip. Having to raise at least part of the money is an experience in giving that is good for them.

When preparing your trip budget, be as inclusive as possible. Try to think of all the possible expenses you could encounter. Even if you can't be exact, make an educated guess and leave room for costs to increase unexpectedly. Items you may need to consider include: transportation costs, meals (on-site and on-road), insurance, study materials, first-aid supplies, work supplies, promtional costs, leaders' expenses, and the like.

Another part of the initial planning is to consider how you will promote the workcamp. After one or two successful workcamps you will probably not have to do much promotion as the quality of the experience will speak for itself. But if the workcamp idea is new to your youth group or church, you may have some resistance and considerable inertia to overcome. A pre-promotion step is to get the support of your pastor and church governing body. Use that support to help increase the credibility of the trip. One of your first efforts at promotion should be a parents' meeting where the youth group and their parents are invited to hear details of the trip and ask any questions they might have. If possible, show slides of the worksite. This will give everyone a better idea of the nature of the project. Be ready for questions about health, safety, and other potential problems. To help alleviate parental fears, have good contingency plans thought out for possible emergencies. Other good promotional methods to help generate interest include informational brochures, bulletin announcements and posters.

Try to inform people about as many details as possible. People have a fear of the unknown, and a dissemination of the facts will answer many questions before they are asked. It is important to emphasize commitment. Non-refundable deposits, official applications, and letters of acceptance are a few ways to emphasize to students the fact that they are committing themselves to serious work.

Many workcamp leaders like Paul Borthwick of Grace Chapel in Lexington, Massachusetts, have rigorous requirements for workcamp participants. These requirements are based on the theory that when much preparation is required, much more is gained from the experience. He recommends that participants write a preparation essay concerning their relationship to God and their hopes and expectations for the trip, plus a follow-up essay on what they learned from the workcamp experience. It is also a good idea to have team meetings to build relationships and improve the working skills which will be needed on the projects. Whatever requirements you make, be sure they are related to the nature of the project. Emphasize that their purpose is to prepare the students for the serious work ahead.

Preparing for the Trip

In most cases, a workcamp involves arranging transportation. It isn't easy to get a large number of people and their luggage from one place to another. In making a decision about transportation, remember that the best way for one group might not work for another. Consider the following factors: safety, distance, cost, need for on-site transportation, number of persons, amount of luggage and equipment, availability, and whether the mode of transportation helps fulfill the objectives of the trip. Some groups use public transportation, some charter buses or use church buses. Others rent or borrow passenger vans. If you decide to use a bus, it is helpful to also take along a truck or passenger vehicle for the short trips you have to make such as to the doctor or grocery store while on site.

However you decide to travel, be certain that your insurance coverage is adequate for the trip. There are two possibilities. Either make sure your church policy covers the participants or make each student responsible for his or her own personal health coverage. If the latter course is taken, you will still need to make sure the transportation is insured and the church is covered for liability. Whatever you do, it is important to get it in writing before you go.

Another major logistic to consider is that of feeding your group. The task should not be looked upon as mere drudgery for it often provides a good opportunity for group members to interact and have fun at mealtime. Even if you choose to divide up food preparation and responsibilities among the students, it is a good idea to have an adult advisor in charge of coordinating the schedule and making sure the necessary items are on hand. Ted Witt, in his booklet, "Workcamping," suggests the following questions to be considered:

1. What cooking facilities are available (how many stoves, ovens, refrigerators, etc.)?
2. How will the available cooking equipment and facilities affect the menu?
3. How will cooking and clean-up tasks be assigned and rotated among the members of our group?
4. How far is it to a supermarket?
5. What kind of cooking utensils are there (size, number)?
6. Are there adequate dishes, silverware, etc.?

For a workcamp to be a positive experience, it is essential that the food be edible and plentiful. Prior planning and shopping for bargains will save money and give you more free time during the work week.

Before you leave for a workcamp, it is important that the leaders be adequately prepared for the project ahead of them. If they have confidence in you and in their own ability to lead, that attitude will be communicated to the students. Perhaps the most vital part of leadership education is "flexibility training." I have never seen a work project where something did not go awry: a van breaks down, the power goes off, the accommodations were not what was expected, the building materials fail to arrive on time, you run out of supplies. Even the most fastidiously planned work project is bound to run into snags, so it is vital that the leaders learn to roll with the punches. An adult leader who becomes angry or discouraged can sour the whole group. It has been my experience that adults have a much more difficult time being flexible than do teen-agers.

Perhaps one of the best ways to train leaders in flexibility is to do role-plays that deal with potential problems. You can have adults act out how they would respond to a transportation breakdown, discipline problems, or work slowdown. Another possible area for leadership training is in basic relational skills: how to deal with a crisis, how to draw youth into conversation, how to lead a discussion, and so on. They should also be trained in practical matters such as travel tips, financial procedures, and work skills.

Finally, in order for a workcamp to function smoothly, it is vital that the group be well-prepared and able to relate to each other in a positive way. It is important that participants understand the objectives of the trip and begin to develop into a caring, Christian community that exercises love as a the rule of life. Well in advance of departure, there should be group orientation meetings which could include:

1. Relationship building among group members.
2. Reviewing goals and objectives.
3. Showing slides and acquainting participants with the project.
4. Learning about the history of the recipient project.
5. Reviewing the work which needs to be done.
6. Developing a covenant of rules and policies for group life on the trip.
7. Reviewing itinerary and schedules.
8. Discussing what to take and what not to take on the trip.

Some groups hold numerous pre-trip meetings while others use a one day or weekend format for orientation. The frequency and magnitude of this operation will depend upon the nature of your trip and the needs of your group. But remember that this kind of proper preparation often makes the difference in the quality of the workcamp experience.

At the Project

The hardest part of any workcamp is the preparation that leads up to it. If the planning has been done well, the week should flow relatively easily. The main concern during the project will be to keep good lines of communication open and to adjust to the unplanned variables which inevitably come up. A daily leaders' meeting is a good way to make sure all problems are addressed. At such a meeting you can deal with any personality conflicts, schedule or work changes, or discipline problems.

The evening hours provide a good opportunity to strengthen the fellowship of the group. Provide a group meeting each night as a way for everyone to come together and share the day's experiences. If you are outdoors, this could be done around a campfire. Singing, sharing, Bible study and prayer are an excellent way to close the day. Make sure the group gets to bed early enough so that they get plenty of rest.

It is often possible to combine a workcamp with a few fun activities as well. If you are near a beach or lake, or have access to a softball diamond or gymnasium, you can allow some time for recreation. It is best, however, to give the work project itself the utmost priority. If you are also going to include sightseeing or a trip to an amusement park, make sure that it does not interfere with the primary purpose of the trip.

In most cases, a workcamp will involve a certain amount of direct contact and interaction with the people who are benefiting from the workcamp. There may be an opportunity for your young people to get to know these people and to learn something about their culture and way of life. If possible, try to involve the local people in the project, working with them in a spirit of cooperation rather than in a paternalistic way. Your young people should be instructed to respect the feelings, values, and rights of the local people and to treat them with humility and love.

One thing to avoid during the week is setting work goals that are unattainable and letting expectations get out of hand. If you set your sights on finishing an entire building but only complete the foundation, there could be unnecessary disappointment. It is best to set realistic goals that are within the capabilities of the group. Tangible results such as a wall built or house painted will provide a great sense of satisfaction that the young people can take home with them.

After the Trip

After you have returned home, it is a good idea to spend some time evaluating the trip and sharing the experience with your congregation. Have everyone who participated fill out an evaluation form and then bring everyone together to explore how the trip could be improved for next year. To interpret the trip, give a complete report to the pastor and the church governing board. The parents and the congregation can be invited to a special program in which the young people tell their experiences, show slides, and thank those who supported them. One group sold "stock" in their project to adults before the trip (see the "Bullish on the Youth Group" idea in Chapter Six); after the trip they held a "stockholders meeting" to show "investors" how their money had been used.

Remember to be sensitive to those in your group who were unable to participate. Because of jobs, family vacations, and other factors, not everyone will be able to go on a project. An intense workcamp experience will do wonders to strengthen and draw together its participants, but it can also alienate those who could not go. This need not be the case if the group leaders and workcamp participants are sensitive to the feelings of those who could not go and make a concerted effort to be inclusive.

A successful workcamp is one of the most difficult yet rewarding experiences you can have in youth ministry. It is a direct purposeful learning experience which can affect people's lives at a very deep level. Some results I have observed include a greater understanding of the mission of the church and the meaning of Christian servanthood, a closer sense of fellowship and love, an increased world awareness and heightened gratitude for the many blessings we enjoy but take for granted.

The gospel message makes clear that we as Christians are to be the body of Christ carrying on God's task of reconciliation and service to the

Someone once said that "God is everywhere lookin' for hands to use." There is probably no better way to use those hands than through a youth workcamp project.

Author's note: I would like to thank Steven Mabry, Paul Borthwick, Ted Witt, Malcolm McQueen, and Dave Wilson for their assistance in putting together material for this chapter.

Bill McNabb is Minister of Youth and Education at Brentwood Presbyterian Church in Los Angeles, California, and is an associate staff of Youth Specialties Ministries.

Chapter Five

Ways for Young People to Impact the Political System

by Anthony Campolo

This chapter contains ideas that allow a group to potentially alter the very structure of society. These ideas involve interaction with the economic and political power structures of the world. They attempt to influence those structures so that they function in accord with what the group believes to be the will of God.

In many Third World countries, this type of social action has radically expressed itself in the revolutionary movements aimed at displacing totalitarian regimes with democratically elected governments. These revolutionaries argue that the existing political and economic structures have become so diabolical that they are beyond reformation. They believe that the rulers of society have organized their power in such a way to prohibit all attempts to change them into just and equitable forms. They have diminished the humanity of their people, and have perpetrated such awesome evil that they have forfeited their right to endure. Those who have adopted this point of view believe that it is not only a Christian right but a Christian imperative to work for the demise of such systems. Equipped with what is usually called "liberation theology," they commit themselves to revolutionary political movements which promise a new socio-economic order which will end oppression.

This book makes no attempt to follow that line of thought and action. However, there are many effective ways for Christians, especially Christian young people, to effect changes in the political and economic structures of their society in legitimate and nonviolent ways.

The ideas presented in this chapter are not attempts to operate out of a position of power, coercion, or force, but simply ways to bring about positive social change.

This kind of social action should not be seen as a substitute for service projects that minister directly to the needs of hurting people. It is vitally important that Christians be involved in ministry to those who are suffering and who are oppressed. This is our highest priority. But there is also truth in the belief that it does little good to minister to the victims of an evil system while doing nothing at all to change that system so that it produces fewer victims. History has demonstrated that, in many cases, when a human casualty of a corrupt system is rehabilitated, that system only produces a dozen more casualties to take the rehabilitated person's place.

Ron Sider, a popular author and leader of Evangelicals for Social Action, sets forth the following parable:

A group of devout Christians once lived in a small village at the foot of a mountain. A winding, slippery road with hairpin curves and steep precipices without guard rails wound its way up one side of the mountain and down the other. There were frequent fatal accidents. Deeply saddened by the injured people who were pulled from the wrecked cars, the Christians in the village's three churches decided to act. They pooled their resources and purchased an ambulance. Over the years, they saved many lives although some victims remained crippled for life.

Then one day a visitor came to town. Puzzled, he asked why they did not close the road over the mountain and build a tunnel instead. Startled at first, the ambulance volunteers quickly pointed out that this approach (although technically quite possible) was not realistic or advisable. After all, the narrow mountain road had been there for a long time. Besides, the mayor would bitterly oppose the idea. (He owned a large restaurant and service station halfway up the mountain.)

The visitor was shocked that the mayor's economic interests mattered more to these Christians than the many human casualties. Somewhat hesitantly, he suggested that perhaps the churches ought to speak to the mayor. After all, he was an elder in the oldest church in town. Perhaps they should even elect a different mayor if he proved stubborn and unconcerned. Now the Christians were shocked. With rising indignation and righteous conviction they informed the young radical that the church dare not become involved in politics. The church is called to preach the gospel and give a cup of cold water. Its mission is not to dabble in worldly things like social and political structure.

Perplexed and bitter, the visitor left. As he wandered out of the village, one question churned round and round in his muddled mind. Is it really more spiritual, he wondered, to operate the ambulances which pick up the bloody victims of destructive social structures than to try to change the structures themselves?

Of course, not all efforts to change the system will get results. Sometimes it will seem like everyone's time was wasted and that nothing at all was accomplished. That is why it is important to keep in mind that one of the best results of any social action is the raising of consciousness that the project brings about in the lives of the young people and everyone concerned. Young people who carry out a social action program develop a commitment to social justice that could have been gained in no other way. As Christians, they are made aware of Biblical and theological imperatives for the kind of changes that they are working to achieve. They become zealous advocates of their causes, and communicate their concerns to a wide range of people who would otherwise have paid little or no attention to them. In many cases, a social action project will get significant public attention. The press may write stories about what is being done and why. Television stations may carry live reports. Public controversy may arise over their activities, making a social concern a topic of widespread community discussion.

But it is not at all unusual for people in power who are challenged by Christian social action groups to undergo changes which lead them to take new positions and to re-think their practices and policies. These people may not take the exact positions advocated by the group which challenged them, but they may modify their positions significantly in the direction of justice and righteousness. Conflict with a social action group often leads those in power to reject their original position and end up with a new stance which is a synthesis of their original viewpoint and that held by their opponents.

When choosing from the following suggestions, remember that only the idea is presented here. Compared to all that may be involved in making the idea work, what appears here may only be "the tip of the iceberg." Whatever you decide to do should be researched thoroughly and carefully planned.

Make sure your group has been adequately prepared and properly motivated for action. There are some projects that only mature or very serious-minded young people will want to tackle. You will need to inform parents and church leaders of the actions you are taking and enlist their support. You will need to be sensitive to the needs of individual group members and to make sure that everyone is enthusiastic about being involved.

Once your group feels confident that they have been led by God to get involved in the political system and once your preparation has been completed, you can expect to see some tremendous things happen in the lives of your young people as well as in society.

THE IDEAS

Campaign Workers

As election time draws near, contact the candidate of your choice and volunteer to work in the upcoming campaign. This work may include delivering literature, making phone calls, developing position papers and making posters. Every party organization in the country is understaffed. Your offer to help will be accepted with wild enthusiasm. Party people will be willing to listen to you; they will be willing to make significant concessions to you and significantly modify party plans and programs to bring them into accord with your viewpoints. Party leaders know that there are too few workers available. They will try to do whatever is necessary to keep hard workers in their camp. When the primary concern of party leaders is to win elections, they will do what they have to do and take those stands which they must in order to secure the kinds of workers who will help them to win. That's why a handful of people can significantly affect party policy.

Candidate's Night

A youth group should consider setting up a Candidate's Night for the entire church or a group of churches. Invite in all of the candidates and give them an opportunity to present their platforms and to answer questions. You will be amazed at how willing candidates are to take advantage of such an opportunity. Tell them you will be inviting the press to be present for the gathering. By doing this, you can call the candidates from both parties into accountability for their decisions, their thoughts, and their voting. You can make them aware that the Christian value system is one which they will have to consider seriously as they engage in political decision making.

Committee Person

As soon as a young person reaches the age of eighteen, he or she can run for the office of "committee person" in his or her local precinct. In most cases an individual will run unopposed because the position is thankless and it offers very little public recognition to the individual who holds the office. However, committee people wield tremendous influence. They are the ones who determine which candidates the party eventually runs for office. No one would be able to become a candidate for the United States Congress, for example, if that individual failed to gain the support of the people on the committee level. Every politician knows that primary elections are won by committee people. Committee people usually determine who carries the party banner in the general elections. Check it out.

Common Cause

Members of a youth group should consider joining the local chapter of Common Cause.. This is a "watchdog" organization established on the national level under the direction of James Gardner. Common Cause exercises great influence on how local campaigns are conducted. This organization also brings candidates to a level of accountability on political issues which have bi-partisan support and which have a great effect on the destiny of the country. Common Cause affects decisions on such things as ecology, military spending, "sunshine laws," human rights, etc. Most Common Cause groups are organized in accord with U.S.

Congressional Districts. To find out who heads up the Common Cause chapter in your Congressional District, you should write to the Washington headquarters, 2030 "M" St., N.W., Washington, D.C. 20036.

County Government Meetings

Members of a youth group should consider attending meetings of the county government. Generally, the officials ask for comments from those who are in attendance. Usually very few people do attend (except when a major issue is being debated) and if you are there you will probably be given the right to speak. If this is not generally part of the practice of the government meetings in your area, ask for the privilege of speaking prior to the meeting. In almost every case you will be given the right to speak on those crucial issues about which you feel strongly. Usually you can find out in advance what the agenda for the day is going to be and the approximate time that a particular issue is going to be handled. If the group carefully prepares its position and has someone speak on it with clarity, the county officials or supervisors will take you very seriously. It is an exciting thing to have the opportunity to be heard by those who shape policies and have a considerable amount of power. This is what "free speech" is all about.

Delegates to the National Convention

In the year of a presidential election, a young person who is of age, could seek election as a delegate to the national convention of that party to which he or she feels strong affiliation. It is best to be elected as an "at large" delegate rather than being committed to any particular candidate. Major political figures scramble for delegate votes as the campaigning culminates in the nominating of a presidential candidate. Those who win as delegates "at large" will find that all the major candidates for the presidency will contact them personally by phone. In these conversations, the individual will be able to air a strong witness for Christ with respect to the kinds of policies he or she wants to see enacted by any presidential candidate to whom support is given. It is amazing how easy it is to win a delegate seat.

Fast for Justice

There may be a bill on the floor of Congress dealing with a particular injustice that has created great oppression, or a piece of legislation that is of great importance for the preservation of human life. For instance, there might be a bill to deliver food to the hungry of India. In response to this, a group of young people can get together and sign a pledge to fast for a few days to show sympathy for the bill. This is very impressive and can effect a tremendous influence. Of course, this has little impact unless the press is notified through well-written press releases. A small group of college students at Eastern College gained national recognition during the Vietnam War simply by fasting to demonstrate opposition by some Christians to what appeared to be a senseless slaughter of human life.

Keep in mind that this kind of action is not fun and games. It is not easy to actually fast for more than a day or so. Your young people should know this and feel committed enough to stick with it for the duration. Any hunger fast should have complete parental support and good medical supervision. It is important that those who do this sort of thing not identify themselves as members of a particular church. They should give themselves a title such as "Coalition for Christian Justice." In this way people in the church who may not agree with your stand will not think you are presuming to speak for them.

Guerrilla Theatre

When there is a great social injustice, a group of young people can develop what has come to be called "guerrilla theatre." This is usually a short play or skit that can be performed in the streets, on the steps of the state capital, or at a city hall. Guerrilla theatre dramatizes the social injustice which the group wants to see corrected. A few years ago, a group of Eastern College students opposed to torture in Iran got a permit to stage a demonstration on the steps of the capitol building in Washington. This demonstration simply dramatized the kinds of torture that were being employed by the government of Iran against political dissidents. The demonstration appeared in the newspapers and got significant public recognition.

Hold a Youth Conference

If your youth group feels strongly about an issue in the upcoming election, or any issue of concern, organize a youth conference dealing with that particular issue. It could be held on a weekend, on a Saturday, or on

Sunday afternoon. Invite in special speakers and advertise the conference well. Write up press releases and see that they are sent to the local news media. After the conference is over, issue additional press releases that describe the decisions that the group made and the positions it took on the crucial issues under discussion. You will be surprised at the receptivity of the media to this sort of thing. Very often, local television stations will send out film crews to cover such events. It's a great way to inform and to motivate young people concerning issues of importance.

Letters to the Editor

On crucial political issues, write letters to the editor of your local newspaper. These are usually published and read by hundreds, sometimes thousands of people—including candidates and policymakers. By doing this you will have a significant forum for expressing your political views from a Christian perspective. Remember you should not sign the letter in such a way that it looks like it comes from your entire group or church. This is not honest or fair to those who may not share your views.

Letter Writing Campaigns

Never underestimate the importance of organizing a letter-writing campaign on an important social-political issue. Congressmen and candidates for office are very much influenced by the flow of mail. A hundred letters on a particular issue can easily sway the opinion of a Congressman or Congresswoman who does not have strong convictions on a particular matter. Make sure that the letters do not have a "sameness" to them. They should all address themselves to the issue and state whether they are for or against a particular piece of legislation, but each person who writes should do so in an individualistic fashion.

Bread for the World is one organization that attempts to keep Christian people aware of important legislation affecting the poor and needy of the world. It encourages churches to send an "Offering of Letters" to local congress people to influence them in the right direction. Even though in some cases the volume of mail may be too great for the congressperson to actually read, a careful record is always kept of letters "for" or "against" every issue. Voting is then done on the basis of that record.

Lobby Groups

It is possible for individual Christians who have a common concern to organize as a lobbying group. Ask your state legislator to register the group as an official lobbying group in your state. The members of the group will then be issued cards designating them as such. This will grant them the right to confront state legislators in order to influence their voting patterns. A group of students at Eastern College calling themselves "The Christian Coalition" has had a significant influence upon the decision-making process of the state legislature in Pennsylvania.

Nominate Your Candidate

In any county or township election, there are usually offices for which the minority party cannot get candidates to run. If someone of proper age in your group is interested in politics, encourage him or her to get a candidate petition and run for one of these offices. By running an effective campaign for a relatively minor office, a candidate, and those who are working with him or her, can establish tremendous political credibility and be in a position to significantly influence party policy and the direction of government.

Party Politics

In almost every county in the United States, both the Democrats and the Republicans have established party organizations. Usually these organizations have youth divisions. In the Democratic Party, it is the "Young Democrats"; and in the Republican Party, it is the "Young Republicans." Christian young people can contact the county chairpersons of the party of their choice and offer to become members of the youth division. In many cases, if not most, the youth division will not be organized. If that is the case, your young people might offer to organize a division and recruit members for it. Either the offer to join an existing organization or the offer to organize a youth division for the party will be received with tremendous enthusiasm by the party leader. A group of only five or six young people joining an existing division will probably be able to determine decision-making policies for such an organization, provided they are loyal in attending meetings and are willing to work hard during political campaigns. Outsiders to politics have no way of knowing how significant the youth organizations of political parties can be. Old pros will involve them in the highest echelons of party decision making. They are often used as a showpiece at party functions and in return, the youth are able to influence the direction of the party in ways that stagger the imagination.

Pass a Resolution

Whenever you are part of a youth convention (like a denominational state youth convention), introduce a resolution of significant political importance which warrants a response from Christians. Get a vote from the convention and then notify your congressman or legislator, as the case may be, of the resolution which the convention has passed. Also prepare a press release and have each young person release the press release to his local paper. The press release could include the name of the young person. For example, "Johnny Jones, while attending the annual meeting of the Michigan Baptist Youth Convention in Flint, Michigan, this past weekend, supported a resolution to. . ." Such personal endorsements of resolutions passed by a denominational group of young people are given serious consideration.

Pickets for Christ

Every political party has annual meetings, dinners, or gatherings of some sort. If the party has ignored a particular issue that is of great concern to your group, or if they have taken a stand that is contrary to what your group understands as the Christian position, then picket that gathering. Get the group together, map out a strategy, spend a day making signs and banners, print up some press releases, and take a real stand for the issue. You will undoubtedly get coverage on radio, television and the newspapers. This will give you even more of an opportunity to express your views on important issues and to explain why your Christian commitment has led you to your position. Sometimes the small amount of persecution that is involved (there will undoubtedly be those who disagree with you) will help young people to solidify their beliefs and strengthen the unity of the group.

Besides political gatherings, the group may choose to picket elsewhere, for example, at a business that engages in unfair labor practices or which builds nuclear weapons, or at an X-rated theatre. In fact, there may be an instance when even a church will take a position on something that is obviously contrary to Scripture. For example, a church may vote to exclude blacks from membership. In such a case, a Christian youth group should not be reluctant to picket the Sunday morning worship service of that church. If we are going to call political and economic systems to repentance, then we must also call the insitutional church to repentance when it sins. When churches are picketed, that's big news, and you can be sure the ramifications and impact will be far-reaching.

Some people may oppose such demonstrations, claiming that Christians should neither intimidate others into doing God's will nor try to elicit support for their positions by a display of power. Those of the Mennonite or Anabaptist tradition, for example, may exhaust themselves in responding to the needs of people on a personal level, but will have no part of an active political effort. They argue that Christians should never deal from a position of power; that the loving witness of sacrificial self-giving is the only Christian means of bringing about social change.

On the other hand, there are others who feel that Christians should collectively stand up for what they believe to be right. They contend that if such demonstrations of conviction can be carried out without violence and without breaking the law, then it is not only right for Christians to do so, but it is their obligation to stand up for Jesus in this way.

You will need to weigh these arguments carefully and to allow your group the opportunity to choose for themselves the action that they take. Nothing should be done on impulse, or just to make waves. Sensationalism and radicalism are not the objective, but rather, doing the will of God.

Position Paper Writers

Candidates for state or national office, if they are not incumbents, do not have staffs to help them develop and write up position papers on crucial issues. A group of intelligent Christian young people can present themselves to a candidate and offer to serve in that capacity. Can you imagine the influence to be had by actually formulating the position that particular candidates will be assuming in crucial legislation?

School Board Meetings

Attend all school board meetings in your local district. Very few citizens ever attend these meetings, and a group of Christian young people who show up and express their views will be able to exercise tremendous influence upon the decision-making processes of the school board. Students are almost always welcomed at these gatherings.

Speak Up at Committee Hearings

When a major piece of legislation is up for discussion and a vote at the state government level, there are usually hearings held by the committee which is handling the bill. By contacting your state legislator you can find out when the committee will hold its hearings. Attend them, speak to the issues, and declare what you believe to be the will of God on those issues. You will be surprised at how open such meetings are to your input, and you will be amazed at the difference your input will make in the eventual formulation of the policy. You don't have to be of voting age to participate in such hearings, but participation in such a hearing may require that you miss school for a day in order to go to the state capital. Generally, high school students are thrilled by that prospect.

The United States Congress also offers an opportunity for special interest groups to speak to issues. When a committee schedules a hearing, ask for permission to attend and to speak to those issues about which you feel strongly. It is important that you incorporate your group into a formal organization with a title, so that you do not come simply as "interested citizens." On one occasion, a group of only thirty young people was able to have significant input upon the development of Congressional legislation concerning civil rights. The group appeared under the title of "Christian Young People Concerned for Racial Justice." The United States Congress allowed this ad-hoc committee to have a speaker address the Congressional committee for more than half an hour. This was one of the most exciting and worthwhile events in which the group had ever participated.

Taking Stock in Corporations

It is important to understand that much political power is exercised by large corporate structures. Huge multi-national corporations exercise tremendous influence upon the destiny of our nation as well as of nations around the world. The assets of these companies make them larger than most governments of the world. Christians often feel that these economic units are too large to be influenced by small Christian groups, but such an assumption is wrong. Christians can pool some money and buy stock in any large corporation which has practices that they want to challenge.

The group can then contact the chairperson of that corporation and ask that a resolution be introduced at the next stockholders meeting. The resolution might, for example, call the company to correct the practices that have been responsible for suffering and injustice. In the resolution itself, one can even set forth the Biblical passages and principles which warrant the resolution. By law, the president of the corporation is obligated to send out your statement to every stockholder prior to the meeting so that each might exercise a proxy vote. Because of this, you are able to create among stockholders an awareness of the social injustice which the corporation is perpetuating.

The next step would be to send someone to the stockholders meeting in order to personally present the resolution and speak on its behalf. Large corporations respond to such action. Often the executives want to effect the kinds of changes which you are demanding, but they believe that the stockholders won't go along with the changes. You may be able to encourage the stockholders to do those things which many of the executives wanted to do all along.

A few years ago, Tom Skinner and some other prominent black leaders decided to bring about changes in policy at General Motors. No one would argue with the fact that the corporate policies of General Motors significantly influence millions of people throughout the world. Their hiring practices, investment policies, and production programs determine who will be employed and what salaries will be paid. Where General Motors establishes production plants may determine which nations or states gain economic benefits. Governments around the world can be influenced by the decisions made by such a huge corporation.

These leaders decided that improvements in the economic status of black people could be brought about if certain changes were made in the policies and practices of General Motors. They secured stock in this corporation and attended its annual stockholders meetings. When they confronted the leaders of the corporation with their ideas for change, they were no longer people who were outside the system pleading for change. By virtue of their stockholdings, they were part of the system, and had the right to be heard and eventually alter the policies of General Motors. This small group became one of the forces that eventually led to the election of Leon Sullivan, a prominent black Philadelphia pastor, to the Board of Directors of General Motors. Dr. Sullivan's influence eventually led to an alteration of the employment practices of General Motors in South Africa. He also initiated a plan that led to General Motors dealerships for black people in black communities. This small group of Christians had a tremendous impact upon the way in which General Motors functioned in Third World countries and in ghetto communities.

There Ought To Be a Law!

Your group may be aware of some social injustice which could and should be corrected by legislation. Get the help of a lawyer, perhaps one within the church, and write up a law that you would like to see enacted. Give it to the representative from your district, who is in the state legislature, and ask him to introduce this piece of legislation on your behalf. Point out that if he will not do this, you will ask the support of the opposition candidate for the same legislation. You will be amazed at how receptive state legislators are to this kind of offer. It is a thrilling thing to see a piece of legislation enacted, which your group initiated, formulated, and introduced to your state legislator.

Chapter Six

Raising Funds for Social Action

Introduction by Wayne Rice

Fund-raising is not ordinarily thought of as a service project, but it can be a very effective and important one. There are many needs that can be met by providing the financial resources to "make it happen." There are thousands of dedicated people serving Christ at home and abroad who would be unable to continue were it not for individuals and groups supporting them financially. There are agencies like World Vision and Food for the Hungry who depend upon the gifts of concerned, caring Christian people to do important relief work all over the world. Additionally, there are many needs right at home, like the poor family down the street or the nearby orphanage or rescue mission, where funds can be applied directly. While it is important to give young people the opportunity to serve others in a personal way, the importance of fund-raising should never be underestimated. Adults usually can reach into their wallets or their bank accounts when they feel led to give to the needy, but most young people are not in the position to do that. They can, however, give of their time and energy to a project which will result in the accumulation of a significant amount of money. The fundraisers in this book are designed to do just that. They involve the youth as a group in activities which will make money. Some are more "gimmicky" than others, but they all have merit if done properly and with the right motivation. Below are some guidelines which may be helpful to you as you choose and plan your next fund-raising activity.

1. Be sure the group understands fully how the money is going to be used. Be as specific as possible. Rather than simply raising money for "hungry people," try to focus in on *particular* hungry people. Identify the country, the city, the village, the tribe, or even a particular family if you can.

If possible, allow your group to visit the place where the money will be used. Let them meet the people and see the situation for themselves. There is no substitute for first-hand knowledge. When kids really understand why the money is needed, they will be highly motivated to work hard and to make the fund-raiser as successful as possible.

If you are giving money to an agency of some kind, ask them to provide you with brochures, photos, films and other information that might be helpful. In some cases, a representative will come and share with the group the work that is being done by that agency. Also, it is never out of line to ask for the agency's financial statement so that the group can see exactly how the money is spent.

2. Consider the possibility of continuing your financial support for a project over a period of several years. Most groups have the tendency to jump from one cause to the next, not realizing that in some cases more harm is done than good. For example, if money is raised to build an orphanage in Haiti, money will also be required for many years in order to pay the operating expenses of that orphanage.

Decide upon the particular project you want your group to support and then make a commitment to it for a period of several years. You can keep in touch with the people you are supporting, get progress reports, watch your money at work, and let them know that they can count on your continued support.

3. Allow the young people to give their own money to the project in addition to the money that they raise with the fund-raising activity. Most kids are not rich, but they usually have a lot more discretionary income than one would think. Have them put up some of their own money. This will help them learn what it means to give of their own resources before asking others to do the same.

4. Limit most of your fund-raising to "worthy" projects, like feeding the hungry, building a hospital, providing supplies for a missionary, etc. This is especially necessary with fund-raisers that require donations. Most people don't appreciate being asked to donate money to send the youth group to Disneyland, to bring in the famous (and expensive) Christian rock group, or to pay for the ski trip to Colorado. Let the kids earn money for these kinds of things by working or saving their allowances. Perhaps you could set up a "youth employment service" at your church to help kids find part-time jobs after school or on weekends. Another way to provide money for such activities would be to simply make sure they are on next year's church budget.

5. Set a goal. Determine ahead of time how much money is going to be needed and how much can reasonably be raised within the time you have. Be realistic and optimistic at the same time. Don't set the goal so high that it will discourage the group, but set it high enough to challenge and motivate them.

6. One of the nice things about fund-raisers is that almost anyone can do them. Some young people lack the confidence necessary to participate in service projects that require a high level of commitment or personal involvement. Not everyone is capable of working in a convalescent home, caring for handicapped children, or doing similar kinds of service. Early adolescents in particular need projects that are relatively easy to do and which may be accomplished in a short period of time. Fund-raisers are ideal for getting kids involved in service who might otherwise be uninvolved.

THE IDEAS

ALLEY SALE

For this unique variation of the "garage sale," you will need to find an alley that has four to eight garages on it that you can "borrow." They should all be located on the same alley. Each garage then becomes a different "shop," named according to the merchandise sold in each one. One shop can sell household items, another can sell sports equipment, others can sell antiques, books, clothing, or baked goods. Each shop should be given a clever name (like the shops in a shopping mall) and signs should be posted at each end of the alley calling attention to this "Unique Shopping Experience."

Preparation for this event is obviously crucial to its success. You will need to enlist many people to donate items to sell. Merchandise will have to be collected, sorted, and priced. Advertising will need to be done (newspaper ads, public service announcements on the radio, etc.). Workers will be needed on the day of the sale to park cars, direct traffic, and do the actual selling. The atmosphere should be as festive as possible. You might even get some musicians to play at one end of the alley and some jugglers or clowns to perform at the other end. Use your own creativity to design an event that will attract the most people possible

If you can't find an alley of this type, then use a normal street, using front lawns or garages off the street. You'll find that this event works so well that you may want to make it an annual event.

AUCTIONS

Why not have an auction? Auctions have been around for centuries and they always seem to draw crowds. There are lots of different ways to do an auction, but the principle is always the same. People are allowed to bid on a variety of items for sale, with the item going to the highest bidder. Sometimes the highest bidder gets a real bargain, but sometimes he winds up paying a lot more than the item is actually worth.

To organize your auction, decide what you want to auction off, ask someone to be the auctioneer, and promote it well. Here are a few "auction ideas":

1. *The Go-For-It Auction:* For this auction, you get businesses and individuals to donate major items to be auctioned off, like cars, appliances, vacation trips, dinners at well-known restaurants, football tickets, and so on. If the cause is a worthy one, items like this are not that difficult to obtain. It takes a lot more work, but usually the return is much greater.

2. *The Junk Auction:* This is just another way to have a garage sale, but it is usually more effective. Get people to donate used items that they no longer want, and then auction them off. Some stuff will be real good;

some will be pretty awful.

3. *The Task Auction:* Get people (including your youth) to donate something that they can do, like mowing a lawn, washing windows, tuning up a car, giving guitar lessons, and the like. Print these tasks up on coupons and then auction them off to the highest bidder. Purchasers may then contact the task-giver to arrange the time that the task will be carried out.

4. *Slave Day:* This is a variation on the Task Auction, but rather than offering specific tasks for sale, you offer each young person for one day who will do any work that the "slave-owner" needs to have done.

5. *The Crazy Auction:* The success of this auction is in the unusual way that the bidding is done. Here's how it works. An article of value is put up for bid and the bidder starts at say, five cents. The person who bid the nickel then tosses in his five cents immediately upon making his bid. The auctioneer announces that the five cent bid has been paid and then raises the bidding to ten cents. The one who bids ten cents tosses in his dime as a firm commitment of his intention. The auctioneer tries to raise the bidding and someone may bid a quarter, whereupon he tosses in the twenty-five cents, making the total in the pot forty cents. The bidding continues until no one bids again, and the article then goes to the last person to bid. All of the previously paid money stays in the pot as well as the final bid. It is easy to sell a pair of shoes for $2.00 when there is actually $11.00 in the pot.

6. *The Gag Auction:* This auction is really just a wild way to take up a collection. Everybody knows in advance that there isn't much of any real value that is going to be auctioned, but it is fun anyway. Everyone is encouraged to bring lots of money so that they can get in on the bidding. People then bid on joke items — like an old toilet seat that is described by the auctioneer as a "unique picture frame," or a "fine seafood dinner" that turns out to be a can of tuna. If the auctioneer is dressed ridiculously, and really gets the audience going, you can raise more money with one of these than with a "real" auction.

BAKE SALES

The traditional bake sale is still a great fund-raiser. All you need to do is ask people in your church or community to donate cakes, pies, cookies, and other baked goods to the youth group and then set up a table in a busy location where the baked goods can be sold. It's an old stand-by idea that always works. There are, however, a couple of other variations of a bake sale that you might want to try:

1.   *The Bake-In:* This is a combination bake sale and lock-in. The youth group gathers at the church at, say, 10:00 p.m. (possibly after a ball game or other activity) to start preparations for the night. All the flour, sugar, eggs, milk and other ingredients should already be in place. These ingredients can be purchased or donated.

Several weeks in advance, the members of the group should be advertising this event and circulating order blanks which list all the items you will be baking. With orders in hand, the youth group spends the night and into the wee hours of the morning baking up all the items that were ordered. Hopefully you can get a few experienced cooks (moms, perhaps) to help out. The next morning, the items can be either delivered or picked up at the church by the purchaser.

One group did this and baked apple and cherry strudel, banana nut bread, doughnuts, coffee cake, cinnamon rolls, white and wheat bread, banana bread, cupcakes, chocolate chip cookies, sugar cookies, banana cream pie, chocolate pie, and more. This will bring great results if you can keep the kids from eating up all the profits.

2.   *The Macho Bake Sale:* Have all the *men* of the church bake pies and cakes and then offer them for sale. Usually it's a lot of fun to see what they come up with. One good way to sell them would be to have an auction, using the rules for the "Crazy Auction" already mentioned in this chapter.

BIBLICAL ICE CREAM FESTIVAL

This fund-raising event can be a lot of fun for your youth group as well as profitable. Essentially the idea is to set up an ice cream parlor with a Biblical theme. Choose a good location, advertise it well, and invite people to try some "heavenly" ice cream dishes created by your group. If possible you should try to get the ice cream donated or purchased at wholesale prices.

Decide on prices for each item—high enough that you will be able to make some money, but not too high. Serve free coffee or punch with each order. Members of the youth group can prepare the ice cream dishes, wait on tables, clean up, and do whatever else needs to be done. You might suggest that they dress up in Biblical garb, just for atmosphere. Something like this can raise a lot of money if the planning is done well in advance and if everyone knows about it.

Here's a sample menu:

~*Menu*~

THE SEA OF GALILEE
A two scoop vanilla island whose shores are washed by a blue-tinted Seven-up ocean.

THE SUNDAY SUNDAE
One scoop of strawberry ice cream surrounded by six teaspoon sized scoops of vanilla ice cream.

PONTIUS PIE
Take command of the situation by ordering a slice of "Pontius Pie": an ice cream and graham cracker spectacular, distinctly Roman.

THE RED SEA SPLIT
A vanilla ice cream trough filled with homemade strawberry topping for those who desire freedom from the slavery of hunger.

SAMSON AND DELILAH
A sensuous scoop of vanilla covered with a seductive topping sharing the dish with a Samson-sized scoop of chocolate ice cream covered with a full head of chocolate chip "hair."

JOSEPH'S CONE OF MANY COLORS
A cone of rainbow sherbet to refresh you on your way to Egypt (or anywhere else).

THE GARDEN OF EATEN
A well coordinated blend of fruity ice cream and toppings, complete with a snake to tempt you to have another.

SHADRACH, MESHACH, AND ABEDNEGO
Three princely kinds of ice cream surrounded by a fiery furnace of red-hots.

JOHN THE BAPTIST
A unique blend of ice cream, honey and locust-shaped almonds to create a most magnificent creation.

TOWER OF BABEL
A towering combination of assorted ice creams, covered with a variety of toppings, whipped cream, and nuts.

PALM SUNDAE
Two scoops of vanilla ice cream, covered with coconuts and enhanced with a decorative palm frond.

BIGGER AND BETTER HUNT

The youth group meets at a central location for instructions. The group is divided into small groups of four or five, who go together on foot or in cars. Each team is given a penny to begin with, and the team is instructed to go to someone's home in the neighborhood and trade the penny for something "bigger and better." They then take the item that they received in trade for the penny to the next house and attempt to trade that item again for something "bigger and better." The team is not allowed to trade for cash. It has to be an item that the person at each house is willing to give in exchange for whatever the team has at that time.

Team members are not allowed to "sweeten the pot" by adding more money to the original penny or any of the items along the way. Each team has one hour (or so), and at the end of the time limit, the teams meet back at the central location and show what they finally ended up with. The group with the "biggest and the best" is the winner. This has been used successfully with many different groups, and some groups have traded for such items as washing machines, watermelons, electric toasters, and even a used car. The items collected can be used later in a rummage sale, or they may be donated to a local service organization.

BIRTHDAY CALENDAR

Design a calendar for the twelve months of the coming year that has on it the birthdates of every member of the congregation, along with important church events. Hunt up some advertisers at $10-$20 per ad (local businesses should be interested), and then sell the calendars to members of the congregation for around $5.00 each. The price, of course, will depend on the cost of the printing and so forth, but you can keep the costs down by using inexpensive methods of printing.

BOOK BLAST

Have the youth group write a book. Really tap the creative potential of the group and have the kids write stories, poetry, articles and essays or submit cartoons, drawings, and anything else that can be reproduced. Then have it all edited by a committee, pasted up and printed by the "offset" process. (Photos can be included this way.) A local printer or bindery can bind them into books. Select a catchy title and design a nice cover which can be printed or silk-screened on cover stock. The books can then be advertised and sold in the church and community as a fine fund-raising project.

BULLISH ON THE YOUTH GROUP

Here's an unusual way to finance your next service project. Print up stock certificates and sell them to members of the church or community as an "investment." Each share can sell for $1.00 with no limit on how many shares a person can buy. Some may want to only buy one share, but others may want to buy a hundred shares. The stock gives them "ownership" in the project and entitles them to attend a "stockholders meeting" so that they can be informed as to how their investment is doing. A "stockholders report" can also be printed. Both the meeting and the report can include photos, testimonies by the kids who participated, a financial statement, and so on. It's an idea that will work.

CALENDAR PAY-OFF

Here's an idea that encourages your kids to be givers. Print up a calendar that has a space for each day of the month. In each space, enter an instruction that will determine how much money they must give that day. The instruction should be humorous, and should vary the amount

Sunday	Monday	Tuesday	Wednesday	Thursday	Friday	Saturday
		1 1¢ For each pair of shoes and sneakers you own.	**2** 3¢ If you disobeyed your parents today.	**3** 5¢ If you forgot to use a deodorant today.	**4** 4¢ If you have BLUE eyes.	**5** 10¢ If you did not clean and straighten up your room.
6 15¢ If you did not attend CHURCH today.	**7** 5¢ If you washed your hair today.	**8** 1¢ For each time you talked on the telephone today.	**9** 5¢ If you got up before seven a.m.	**10** 3¢ If you wore any type of Jeans today.	**11** 1¢ For each soda you drank today.	**12** 2¢ For each hour of sleep you had last night.
13 1¢ For each mile you live away from your church.	**14** 2¢ If you have a hole in your sock.	**15** 5¢ If you did not do your homework.	**16** 2¢ If you have your license to drive a car.	**17** 4¢ If you have BROWN eyes.	**18** 1¢ For each letter in your last name.	**19** 10¢ If you shaved anything today!
20 5¢ If you wore blue today.	**21** 5¢ For each test you had today.	**22** 1¢ For each class you had today.	**23** 50¢ If you were not at Teen Choir tonight.	**24** 10¢ If you did not eat breakfast **at home** this morning.	**25** 3¢ For each time you failed to make your bed this week.	**26** 20¢ If you did not donate any money yesterday.
27 10¢ If you have a pair of Nike's.	**28** 3¢ For each pair of gloves you own.	**29** 3¢ If you didn't read your Bible today.	**30** 10¢ Because it is almost the last day to pay.	**31** 15¢ If you wore the color red today.		

given from one day to the next. When the month is up, the kids bring in the money they owe. At that time you can give awards for who had to pay the most money, the least, the most expensive day of the month, and so on.

A variation of this would be to print the instruction for each day on separate sheets of paper, fold them and staple them, so that they are concealed until the end of each day. The instruction can then be a "fine" for certain things done or not done. For example, it might say "Pay five cents for each class you were late to today," or "Pay twenty-five cents if you forgot to brush your teeth."

Allow a space on the calendar where kids can write in how much they owe each day. They can just total it up at the end of the month. You might add one "extra" space for them to give any amount they choose. This approach adds a little fun and variety to giving.

CARHOP FRY OUT

Have the kids turn the church parking lot into an old-fashioned drive-in restaurant, with carhops on roller skates, greasy hamburgers, and the whole bit. Invite the whole community to come and eat in their cars while the kids serve hamburgers. hot dogs, milk shakes, french fries, etc. Set up a P.A. system that will play oldies but goodies, and make it a wild and crazy night of fun. Charge enough to make a profit and this idea can make an excellent fund-raiser.

CAR WASHES AND MORE!

Car washes are extremely popular as fund-raisers because they usually are easy to organize, a lot of fun for the kids to do, and most people still need to get their cars washed. When in doubt, have a car wash!

The first thing to do is find a good location, like a gas station at a busy intersection (with plenty of room for parking and washing cars). You will, of course, need to get permission and offer to pay for the use of water and electricity for the day. You will also need to line up plenty of kids to do the washing. Kids can sign up to work in shifts.

You will also need to obtain hoses, buckets, nozzles, soap, towels, chamois skins, squeegees, window cleaner, soap pads, tar remover, vacuum cleaners, and so on. It is best to have plenty of supplies on hand.

You will need to make several large attractive signs that are noticeable from the roadway, and also put up some posters around town telling where the car wash location is.

When you are washing cars, make sure your group has a good system so that people don't have to wait a long time for their cars. You should be able to wash a car in about ten minutes, inside and out. Four kids can do the outside while one works on the inside. If you do a good job, and if the kids are courteous, most people will not only pay the price you have set, but will offer to pay more.

It would be a good idea to print up a small flyer that tells about the particular service project that your group is doing to give to the people while their cars are being washed. This lets them know that the money they are spending for the wash is going to a good cause.

Here are some other valuable "tips" relative to car washes:

1. *Sell tickets in advance.* Print up car wash tickets and have your kids out selling them for a week or two before the actual car wash takes place. That way, all the kids are involved, even if they can't personally help wash cars. Also, some people will buy tickets even though they don't expect to bring their car in to be washed. They may just want to help out with the project.

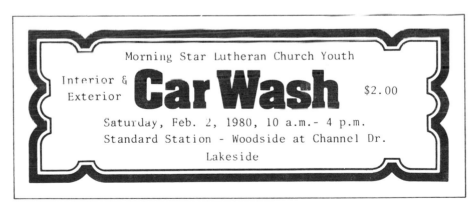

2. *Try getting the use of a commercial "do-it-yourself" car wash.* Every city has several of those car washes that are nothing more than stalls with coin-operated "jet-stream" sprayers that accept quarters. See

if you can get permission to set up there and use that equipment for a flat fee per car washed. Usually your costs will be higher, but you will wind up washing a lot more cars in a shorter amount of time. The management of the place will cooperate if they think you will increase their business for the day, which you most certainly will. It's worth checking out.

3. *Try a Car Wash-a-thon.* Plan a regular car wash, but also encourage people to sponsor your group by pledging a certain amount of money for each car washed during the day. Some people may not want to have their car washed, but they will contribute to the group in this way. If a person pledges ten cents per car, and your group washes a total of 90 cars during the day, that person would then owe the group $9.00. You can set a limit on it for people who are afraid you might wash 1,000 cars.

4. *Try washing other vehicles as well.* If you live close to a harbor, how about having a "boat wash"? Many boat owners would gladly pay to have someone wash down their boats. If you live near a small airport, see if you can secure permission to wash down small private planes. Some groups have done this with good success. Airplane owners will often pay a lot of money to get their plane shined up. You can also wash motor homes, trucks, or you can even wash people's *houses.* One group contracted with the local school district to come in once a month and wash all the school buses. Think of all the possibilities!

5. *Speaking of possibilities, how about windshields?* Service stations don't offer much in the way of "service" anymore, so most people drive around town with dirty windshields. Try setting up at the entrance (or exit) of a busy parking lot and as people come and go, ask them if they would like to have their windshield cleaned. You can do this right on the spot, or while they are shopping. Charge a small amount for the windshield only, or more for all the car windows, inside and out. It's an idea whose time has come.

CHRISTMAS FUND-RAISERS

Christmas is a good time to do fund-raising events for many reasons, but an obvious one is that people are already in the spirit of giving. The giving that is done around Christmas is usually rather superficial and materialistic, however, which makes it an ideal time for your youth to be involved in some kind of mission or service project. The following fund-raising ideas can be used very effectively at that time of the year:

1. *The Christmas Tree of Love:* Place a Christmas tree (either real or artificial) in the church foyer. Put a few decorations on the tree, but leave it embarrassingly bare. Leave a package of ornament hangers under the tree, along with a donation box, decorated to look like a gift. Ask the people of the church to consider hanging one of their Christmas cards on the tree with greetings to the entire congregation as an alternative to sending out individual cards to everyone. The card can be hung on the tree by using one of the ornament hangers provided. Also ask them to donate the money that will be saved by not spending so much on cards or postage to whatever worthy project you happen to have. The money can be deposited in the gift box under the tree. Of course, people can give more than the money they save if they choose.

2. *Youth Gift-Wrapping Service:* This can be done either at the church or at a shopping center. The latter will obviously be the most lucrative, but it is getting difficult to get permission since most shopping centers already have some kind of gift-wrapping service. If it is done at the church, just have the church membership alerted to the service and have them bring in their gifts to be wrapped for a nominal fee per gift.

3. *Christmas-Grams:* A "Christmas-Gram" is a Christmas greeting made by the youth group which can be sold and delivered by the youth group. The first thing to do is to plan a get-together to make them. Have on hand plenty of red and green net (you can purchase this at any fabric shop), red and green yarn, loads of individually wrapped candies, and red and green construction paper. Decide on a shape for your "card" — perhaps a star, a Christmas tree, or a Christmas bell. Cut the construction paper into the decided shape — approximately three inches by three inches. This will be used for people to write their messages. Cut the net into small squares and place two or three pieces of candy inside the net. Tie a piece of yarn around the net. Use a hole puncher to make a hole in the construction paper cut-out and run the yarn through it to attach to the net-wrapped candies. Tie it in a bow. Now you have a "Christmas-Gram." Next, decide on a place in the church to set up a Christmas-Gram booth. Advertise in your church paper and with posters throughout the church. Invite people to buy a Christmas-Gram, write a message on one side of the construction paper cut-out and the name of the persons to whom it is to be delivered on the other side. For a predetermined amount, the youth will furnish the Christmas-Gram and deliver it.

4. *Youth Postal Service:* Let the congregation know that they don't have to mail their Christmas cards locally this year. They can just address them and pay the youth group to deliver them by hand. They can all be delivered on the same day, so the routes can be worked out to save gas. The kids can deliver the cards along with a Christmas Carol for a slight extra charge.

CHURCH JANITORS

One youth group was able to raise a lot of extra money by becoming the church janitors. Something like this provides income for projects on a steady basis and gives members of the youth group something to do after school and on Saturdays. Most churches have to hire someone to do the work — so why not the youth group? It works great and the money can be put to a good cause.

CRAFTS BOUTIQUE

Crafts and handmade items for the home are very popular nowadays. There are probably many people in your church or community who are very talented at making things that would sell in a "boutique" or gift shop. So why not set up a Crafts Boutique to help finance your next mission project? Pick a good location, advertise it well, and invite everyone to make something in the "arts and crafts" motif which they will allow to be sold on a consignment basis. You can buy the items from them at a wholesale price, with the profit going to support your project. Some people may be willing just to donate their craft items outright.

One church did this in a big way, and on one weekend sold over $20,000 worth of goods. A fixed percentage of the income went to a mission project, and the rest went to the people who had made and sold the items. Needless to say, it was very successful.

DINNER THEATRE

Here's a fund-raiser that everyone enjoys. Pick a weekend and get a good location (it could be the church's "fellowship hall") and put on a "Dinner Theatre," featuring good food and a theatrical performance by the youth group. It can be done seriously (with a well-rehearsed play and "gourmet" cooking) or it can be more "tongue-in-cheek," with goofy looking waiters, mediocre food, and some crazy skits and fun entertainment.

The key to the success of your dinner theatre will be adequate preparation and enthusiasm on the part of the youth group. Everybody can get involved, either with the food, the decorations, the publicity, the entertainment, or something. Tickets can be sold for several weeks in advance to insure a "sell-out" crowd for both Friday and Saturday night. One youth group did this and raised over $4,000 in a single weekend. And everybody had a great time.

DONUT SALE

Here's an easy youth group fund-raiser that might work at your church. Have the group bring donuts to church and provide them each Sunday before the morning worship service along with coffee. The donuts can either be donated, bought at wholesale, or homemade. The people then buy the donuts for the going price, just enough that the youth group can make a little on each one sold. Most people really enjoy coffee and donuts in the morning at church, and are happy to pay for them.

DRIVE-IN MOVIE NIGHT

If your church has a big parking lot, or if you have another large area that's useable, here's a great event that can be used as a fund-raiser. Get a large movie screen and set it up on one end of the parking lot. If you have a building adjacent to the parking lot, you might be able to just hang the screen over the side of the building. You will also need a 16mm projector and a few large speakers. And, of course, you will need a movie to show.

You can then have a drive-in movie in your church parking lot and invite all of your church and neighborhood to come. If you are in a heavily populated neighborhood, you may need to check with local ordinances, or with the neighbors, about the potential noise that might be generated. If that is a problem, then you might want to find a parking area that is far enough away from houses not to be a problem.

You can charge admission per car or per person. You can also set up a refreshment stand and sell soft drinks, popcorn and candy. Make sure you do it on a warm night, and encourage people to bring chairs, chaise lounges, and so on. Be sure and book a good film that everyone will want to see, as well as a couple of shorts (like cartoons) and advertise it well. You might even put an ad in the theater section of your local newspaper. With plenty of advance planning and enthusiasm, an event like this can be a real success.

EGG SALE

Some groups have been able to raise a lot of money with this unusual approach. Members of your youth group solicit donations by going door-to-door. They first explain the project to each resident, then ask each person to donate one egg so that the egg might be sold by the youth group. After collecting the egg, the kids go to the next house and ask that resident if they would *buy* one egg to help support the youth group project. At the next house, they collect another egg, and then at the next house they sell it, and so on. You don't need a set price for the egg, as some people will offer a lot more than the egg is worth. Since this fund-raiser needs no initial investment, it is possible to raise quite a bit of money if you have several groups out working.

GOLF CLUB WASH

Here's a fund-raiser that is really unique! Set up a booth at the 18th green of a local golf course and offer to wash golf clubs for the tired hackers. All you need is permission from the golf course pro (or park board for municipal courses), a pail of soapy water, a brush, a pail of clean water, a coin collector, and a few towels. As an extra service, you might want to wax the woods and use a metal polish on the irons. If the money is going to a worthwhile project, most golfers will be glad to pay a reasonable price.

GOLF TOURNAMENT

Some youth programs have had good success with sponsoring golf tournaments in the community. This works best if you are in a large church with a lot of golfers in it, or if you have a way to attract golfers from all over the area. You will need to reserve a local golf course and work out a "deal" on green fees, if possible. Someone with some golf tournament experience will need to organize the tournament itself, establishing the rules, the tee-off times, and so forth. You can line up some nice prizes (donated) for the lowest score, highest score, closest to the pin on the 18th hole, etc. You might want to enlist some "celebrity" type players to host each foursome. The entry fee should be high enough to make it a good fund-raiser, but low enough to attract lots of players. You might want to wrap up the tournament with a banquet where the awards can be presented and the mission project explained.

GRANOLA PARTY

Here's a fund-raiser that most people can really sink their teeth into. Get the youth group together for a "Granola Party" in which the kids make their own special brand of granola to be sold later. Find a good recipe — preferably one that includes lots of "good stuff" like nuts, banana chips, carob chips, coconut, grains, honey, and the like. Have the kids prepare the granola in large quantities, then bag it, put it in decorated coffee cans, and sell it door-to-door or to friends and relatives. A variation of this would be to make and sell jam, preserves, dried fruit, or other "natural" foods.

GROUP GARDEN

This fund-raising project will take plenty of preparation and hard work. Plus, it will require some time before any money is actually earned. Nevertheless, it has great practical value and offers your youth group some rich learning experiences along with the money that is raised.

Locate and obtain permission to use a large plot of suitable gardening land. Perhaps a church member has such an area and would let you use it. The larger your youth group, the more land you will want.

Prepare your youth group garden for planting early in the spring. Seeds may be donated by church members, local stores, or they may be purchased by the youth group. This initial investment is relatively small.

After the garden is fully planted, you wait on it, water it, and work in it! Plan some summer mid-week Bible studies at your garden. Kids should bring their Bibles and hoes. Your Bible studies could be based on Christian growth, the value of work, or even patience!

At harvest time, gather the produce in and sell it. The money earned can be used for your fall service project. Good gardening!

HIRE A SUPERKID

This is basically a kind of "employment service" for your youth group. Most unemployed young people have lots of time on their hands after school and on weekends. You and your church can help them to find good part-time jobs which give them meaningful work and which raise money both for them and for the youth group.

To make it happen, print up an attractive flyer that includes information on all of the "odd jobs" that the kids can do: mow yards, wash cars, babysit, clean house, paint, fix cars, and so on. After printing up the flyers, distribute them throughout the neighborhood and wait for the calls to start coming in. Chances are your response will be very good.

Assign the jobs that come in to the kids according to their abilities and their preferences and give them the responsibility of completing it and doing a good job. If the customer is satisfied, chances are very good that they will become a "regular customer." When the jobs start thinning out a little bit, just send out more flyers or get some other free publicity.

Employers can either pay the young people or pay the youth group. You might want to work out a system where a percentage of the money

HIRE A SUPERKID!

4 Good Reasons You Should!

1. It's been a long, hard winter and you deserve more time golfing, fishing, swimming, or just goofing off in the sun. Don't you agree?

2. Whatever the job, SUPERKID does a super job.

3. SUPERKID is reliable, economical, and of course, very humble.

4. SUPERKID needs money. The crime-busting business is slack in this area, and doesn't pay too well even when it's good. Since SUPERKID is short of summer cash, and since neither begging nor mugging fit his image, he's turning to an old-fashioned, almost archaic solution . . . work!

WHO ARE THE SUPERKIDS?

When they aren't crime-busting, the SUPERKIDS are the mild mannered Teens 'N' Twenties that attend Calvary Temple located at 444 West Grand. Their ages vary from 13 to 28. They are active members of our Teens 'N' twenties program (known as The ARK) and are presently members of our Y.E.S. Group, (Youth Employment Service) that is coordinated by Bruce McCarty.

HERE ARE SOME OF THE JOBS:

LAWN WORK -- Mowing, raking, weeding, trimming, etc.

CAR WASHING -- Or polishing, waxing, compounding, etc.

BABY SITTING -- Lots of experienced baby sitters.

PET SITTING -- It's much cheaper than leaving your pet with a vet.

LAWN WATERING -- While your on vacation.

LIGHT HAULING -- Small truck available to help with any moving needs.

GENERAL CLEAN UP -- Window washing, basement or garage cleaning, etc.

ODD JOBS -- Whatever needs doing, they'll try.

BACK UP HELP -- If it takes more than one or two there are plenty.

CALL NOW!

goes towards the youth group project, and the rest is kept by the young person to be used in any way he or she wants.

A good resource for this is a brochure entitled "How to Get Plenty of Profitable Part-time Jobs for Your Teen-Agers" by Pat Higgins, 1549 Hampton, Grosse Pointe Woods, MI 48236.

INVENTORY

A few phone calls will help you to determine whether or not this idea will work for your youth group. Check with some large retail stores in your city and volunteer to help them "take inventory." Every store must take a periodic inventory, a time of counting and listing every item on their shelves. They usually need temporary help to do it. Some stores now have this performed by computers, but many (especially locally owned businesses) still use real people. It's a one-shot work opportunity that probably will get the kids at least minimum wage. Money raised can go towards the service project of the youth group.

LE GRAND CHATEAU

This fund-raiser is great fun for everyone. The idea is to open "for one night only" your own fine French restaurant — an elegant dining experience that includes "classy" entertainment. The whole thing, however, is done slightly tongue-in-cheek. The catch is the small print at the bottom of the menu which reads: "Management reserves the right to make substitutions without patron consent." So, regardless of what people order, they all get the same thing.

The menu should be elaborate and include extravagant dishes at high prices. It should look like a regular menu (with the exception of the catch line at the bottom, of course). The publicity should include a snooty "reservations only" system, so the right amount of food can be prepared. You can also have a "dress code" (ties for the gentlemen, please). Decorations should be as elegant as possible, with cut flowers, candles, linen on the tables, and classical music playing in the background.

The waiters should be dressed to the hilt, with the maitre d' in tux if possible. The food should be nice but simple: juice, tossed salad, baked chicken, baked potato, vegetable, roll, dessert. The program after the meal can be anything you want. Be sure to allow a few minutes to explain

Le Chateau Grande
~ Entrées ~
Includes dinner roll, dessert, and hot beverage

Storione á la Cardinale   Bigginaccá de Renaldois
$11.55 $8.90

New York Steak   Fischer Fried Chicken
$9.20 $8.75

Veal Marengo and Gamberi   Arthur's Perogy Geschmäck
$13.60 $9.00

Dumpling Dewar Stew   Lobster Waikiki
$5.00 $8.65

(childrens portions available upon request)

~ Appetizers $4.00 ea. ~

Escargot   Galettes au Fromage   Canapes
Frogs Legs   Bongo Bongo

Floor Shows commence at 7:30 & 9:30 p.m.
Management reserves the right to substitution without patron consent

your project and how the proceeds of the evening will be used.

At the close, the waitress can present the "cheque" to each customer. It can instruct people to make their donations in any amount and to pay either their waiter or pay on their way out. Usually a special event like this gets very good results. It's worth all the work involved.

PAPER BOOSTER CLUB

In most areas it is possible to pick up some money by recycling used newspapers. It takes a lot of paper to make it very profitable, but if organized properly, a paper collection can be a good way to raise dollars for your ongoing projects.

Enlist members of the congregation and neighbors to become members of the "Paper Boosters Club." When they join (you can give them an official membership certificate) they promise to save all their newspapers especially for your youth group. Then, once a month, set up a paper collection route for kids to go around and pick up all the paper. If you get enough people involved, you can earn a lot of money in this way. The same can be done with aluminum cans and other items that can be recycled for cash.

PENNY DRIVE

This is a fund-raiser that gets everybody involved. On a given day, you ask people to bring in to the church (or some other collection location) all the pennies that they have been saving over the course of the year. The place of collection should be a large flat floor (like a gym floor) upon which is a large design that the youth group has cut out of paper. The larger the better. The idea is to completely cover the paper design with pennies. It will take thousands of pennies to do this. As the pennies are collected they can be brought in and placed side by side on the paper design. The effect is a kind of mosaic which looks pretty impressive. People can keep returning during the day to see how the design is progressing.

Publicity for an event like this must begin a long time in advance so that people have time to collect all their pennies. Those people who come and contribute other kinds of money (silver or bills) are certainly welcome, but encourage the idea of pennies. Pennies seem very small, but when they are put together with a little commitment — the result is very impressive. Take pictures of the final project for the local newspaper.

PIZZA SALE

Why not set up your own "Pizza to Go" shop for a night, using the church kitchen or some other kitchen where you have access to some large ovens. Some frozen pizza companies and grocers are willing to give substantial price reductions to non-profit organizations. Get some frozen pizzas, or make your own pizzas from scratch and sell them to people in the church. Advertise it well, give the phone number for ordering, and arrange for some kids to be cooks and others to deliver the pizza all over town. It's something that kids will enjoy doing, and if they don't eat all the profits, it can be an excellent fund-raiser. The same thing can be done, by the way, with submarine sandwiches and other "fast food" items.

PLEDGE-A-THONS

One of the most popular ways to raise money these days is the "Pledge-a-thon," in which people are asked to pledge a certain amount of money while kids in the youth group perform some kind of activity. The amount given by the donor will usually depend on the activity and the endurance of the youth group. The activity can be something foolish (like dribbling a basketball) or something worthwhile (like picking up trash along city streets).

The best way to do one of the "Pledge-a-thons" listed here is to give each young person a sign-up sheet (pledge sheet) that can be used to obtain pledges from as many people as possible. If the activity is to be done "by the hour" (with a certain amount to be pledged for each hour), each donor only needs to give a small amount per hour, like twenty-five cents. But if the young person gets twenty people at twenty-five cents per hour, then he will be making $5.00 per hour for performing the specified activity. When the activity is concluded, the young person can contact each donor and collect the appropriate amount.

Here are some "Pledge-a-thons" that have worked well with other groups:

1. *Rock-athon:* Kids meet at the church on Friday night for a weekend of rocking in rocking chairs. They must rock continually, except for a five-minute break each hour to use the restroom. They may read books, watch films, eat snacks, and so on, while they are rocking, but they cannot stop, except at the hourly breaks. Donors pledge a small amount for each hour rocked. Some kids have done this for over 48 hours, without stopping.

2. *Jog-a-thon:* Use a running track and take pledges for each lap that the kids run. Or, use streets and paths (like a marathon course) and take pledges for each mile that the kids run.

3. *Skate-a-thon:* Same as above, only use a skating rink. Probably the best way to take pledges for skating is by the hour, since distance is hard to measure.

4. *Buck-a-Basketball Game:* Have a basketball game between two rival youth groups or two teams within the same youth group. Take pledges from people to give a "buck a basket" scored by their favorite player. A variation of this would be to make the game a marathon game (play as long as possible) and have people pledge a "penny a point" for every point that their favorite team scores. Points could be scored in the thousands.

Another way to do this would be to lower the baskets to nine feet and have a "Dunk-a-thon." People can then pledge for regular points, but pay a higher amount for each "slam dunk" a player makes. Kids like this game a lot. One youth group made over $700 after expenses with this one.

5. *Work-a-thon:* The first step is to find work that needs to be done, preferably for elderly people, handicapped people, or others who could not otherwise pay to have it done. The kids then obtain pledges from people for each hour that they work. The more pledges they get, the higher the hourly wage will be. The money earned goes to support the service project, and some valuable work gets done at the same time.

6. *Trash-a-thon:* This one makes money while cleaning up the environment. Kids hit the streets with big plastic garbage bags and collect as much litter as possible. Pledges are made for the number of bags

of trash they pick up. The only rule is that they cannot take trash out of trash containers. It must be trash that needs to be picked up off the streets, vacant lots, and so on.

One group got a local trash collection service to provide several large "dumpsters" that were placed in the church parking lot. All the dumpsters were filled with trash by the kids, and the congregation was able to see it for themselves on Sunday morning when they arrived for church. The local newspaper ran photos and the event turned out to be an excellent bit of publicity for the youth group. A lot of money was raised at the same time.

7. *Read-a-thon:* This one has also been called a "Bible-a-thon," but the "Read-a-thon" gives you more flexibility. The idea is to get the kids together for some non-stop reading (and listening) for as long as possible. If your group were to start on a Friday night, and continue on until Sunday, they could almost read through the entire Bible.

One person reads from the front of the room (the reading box) while the rest of the group follows along or just listens. The reading job rotates from one person to the next at agreed upon intervals, like every thirty minutes. It would be a great idea to record the reading on cassette tapes, then these tapes could be made available to shut-ins, or people who are unable to read for themselves.

You may want to read something other than the Bible, like some of the great Christian classics. This may have more appeal to the kids. The main thing is that everyone participates, either as reader or listener, for the duration. The money is raised by taking pledges for the number of hours (or pages) that the group reads without stopping. Breaks can be scheduled for using the bathroom, exercise, or snacks.

8. *Starve-a-thon:* This would be ideal for a world hunger emphasis. The kids go on a weekend fast and accept pledges for the number of hours that they go without food. They are permitted fruit juices or water, but no solid food. During the fast, other activities can be scheduled, like games, discussions, films, and so on. World Vision's "Planned Famine" (see Chapter Seven) is a good example of how to go about doing this.

9. *Bike-a-thon:* Like the Jog-a-thon, only do it on bikes. How about a "Trike-a-thon"? Get high school students riding tricycles around a track for a few hours for something that is really fun to watch.

10. *Chain-a-thon:* Here's one for Christmas. Kids make paper chains out of red and green construction paper, or popcorn chains, and take pledges for each foot or yard of chain that they make. Then the chains can be used to decorate the church Christmas tree, or they can be sold for additional funds.

11. *Domino Drop:* By now, we have all seen the incredible domino mazes in which dominoes are placed end to end in a huge design. The domino at the beginning of the design is pushed over and one by one the others fall until all the dominoes have fallen. Many of these designs are so intricate that it takes several minutes for all the dominoes to fall.

Have your youth group get people to pledge a certain amount of money per domino. Then have your group design a pattern of dominoes that will include as many dominoes as they can get their hands on. (They, of course, can practice ahead of time to find the best design possible.) When they have finished their final design of dominoes, they push the first one and watch them all fall. All of the fallen dominoes are counted and then multiplied times the pledge for each domino. This can be a great fund-raiser and a lot of fun for everyone involved.

12. *Pins for Missions:* For this one, secure the use of a bowling alley and set up a bowling tournament or an evening of bowling with your young people. The object is to raise money by taking pledges from businessmen and other adults in the community. Each kid enlists the help of sponsors who pledge a certain amount of money (five cents, ten cents, twenty-five cents or more) for each point scored while bowling. Each kid bowls three games and the total of the points scored in the three games is the number that determines the amount of each sponsor's pledge. In a tournament, the "winners" continue scoring more points, therefore collecting more money for the cause. One group called the event "Pins for Missions" and the money was used for world missions.

RECIPE BOOKS

This one really goes over great in most churches. The first step is to collect "favorite recipes" from all the ladies of the church (and men who like to cook, too). If you collect recipes from forty or fifty people, you will have enough to put together your "official" church recipe book. Send each contributor a form which includes all the facts needed for the recipe:

ingredients, preparation, yield, etc. Each recipe can be named and the name of the "chef" can be included. Then, after printing up the books (they can be mimeographed), sell them back to all the people who contributed and anyone else who wants to see how various people come up with those great dishes at the potluck. It will be a church best-seller.

RUN FOR OTHERS

Running is something that a lot of people do for fun and for good health these days, not just to get somewhere fast. People even pay money (lots of it) to run. They buy running shoes, shorts, sweat bands, magazines on running, and they even pay to enter races. So, why not capitalize on this and have a marathon race of some kind that benefits your next service project. You can call it "Run for Others," or something along that line.

All you have to do is find a course or track, select a suitable day, and then get the word out. The race can be short for kids, longer for adults, and everyone who enters can be given a special t-shirt which bears the name of the race. Set the entry fee high enough to cover expenses (trophies for the winners) plus make some money for the project. Enlist the support of local athletic clubs, the YMCA, etc., and you will be surprised at the response that you get.

SAMPLE FAIR

This idea takes a few months to get ready for, but it is very effective as a fund-raiser and it is different enough to really attract a lot of attention. The first step is to write a form letter (like the one below) to various companies that provide products, foods, or services. This can be sent to nationally known companies or to local companies. You might want to contact some of these personally with a phone call or visit. In the letter, ask them to give you a large quantity of free samples for your "Sample Fair."

If a letter like this is sent to enough companies, you can get hundreds of different free samples for your Sample Fair. Tickets to the Sample Fair can be sold for whatever price you feel is reasonable and your kids can pass out the samples at the Fair, giving one each to a customer. Some companies may provide plastic bags for people to collect things in, or they

```
Dear Sirs:

    Would you like us to promote your product?
    Our senior high youth group has decided to raise money
to purchase a _____ for our church. We are calling
our project a "Sample Fair". In order for us to be a
success, we are asking you to help...and in return we
will be helping you to promote your product.
    Here is our request: Do you have a sample or "pass-out"
item for promotion? This will not be sold. Tickets in
advance and at the door will be sold. Each person will be
entitled to one of each sample. To complete the evening,
the youth will present a "Home Talent Show".
    We're certain the samples will create interest and
excitement and we will have a good turn-out.
    If you are interested and care to help us with your
"Sample", we would be very pleased. We are setting our
goal to sell 300 tickets. This event will take place
on _____ in our church fellowship room.
    Thank you very much.
                                        Sincerely,
```

may send a representative to help explain the product. At any rate, the overhead is low and the benefits are high. You can also provide a refreshment booth and sell baked goods and concessions to add to the festivities. It can be a fun evening that raises a lot of money for a worthwhile cause.

SINGING VALENTINE

This one obviously works best on Valentine's Day. The youth group simply invites each member of the congregation to "purchase" a valentine for his or her "sweetheart" (secretly) on the Sunday before Valentine's Day. You can charge somewhere around $5.00 per valentine. Then, on Valentine's Day, the youth group arrives at the "sweetheart's" house and delivers the surprise singing valentine. The group should all be dressed in red and several members can be dressed as Cupid. The group can either write fun love songs or sing some well-known ones. After singing (which can be both romantic and silly), the sweetheart can be presented with a "Certificate of Affection" with their secret admirer's name on it. This activity can also involve delivery of flowers and/or candy (for extra cost). The elderly and shut-ins especially appreciate receiving a surprise "singing valentine."

SOUP SUPPER

The basic idea here is to prepare lots of soup and have a soup extravaganza that people pay to attend. You can enlist the help of members of the congregation who know how to cook up a pot of delicious homemade soup, and you can create your own special concoctions by combining cans of commercially-prepared soup, adding other ingredients to make the soup unique. Serve salad, bread, something to drink, and provide small cups so the people can sample lots of differernt soups. Charge enough at the door so that the group can turn a little profit for their project. Advertise it well, and the responses should be good.

SPOOK HOUSE

Many youth groups and youth organizations have had real success at sponsoring a "Spook House" or "Haunted House" each year at Halloween. If you can find a good location, you can design a kind of "maze" that kids walk through, from one room to another. Each room features something scary or spooky that fits in with the Halloween theme. A good Spook House takes a lot of work, several months of preparation, good publicity and more, but in most cases the results are worth it. Some organizations raise as much as $50,000 a year with a well-advertised Spook House. For some good ideas on how to create your own special effects and illusions for a very spooky Spook House, see *Ideas Number 23,* published by Youth Specialties.

One caution: It is generally recommended that you avoid extremely offensive exhibits at a Spook House sponsored by a Christian organization. Things like mutilation of the human body, violence, and witchcraft should be avoided. There are lots of scary special effects that can make a Spook House a lot of fun without bringing in the occult and extreme bad taste. Use your own judgment on this.

SPRING CLEANING

Spring is usually a good time for people to clean out their garages, so why not organize it? Pick a weekend or two, and encourage everyone in the church to reserve one of those days to clean out their garage. And for free — one or two members of the youth group will help. In most cases, people uncover all kinds of stuff that they would just as soon get rid of, so they are asked to donate that stuff for a big youth group garage sale. The end result is that everyone gets a clean garage and the youth group gets the proceeds from a good garage sale.

TEA TIME

Sometimes people get tired of youth groups selling tickets, or of going to fund-raising banquets, car washes, bake sales, etc. So here's a different approach. Mail each church member a letter stating, "We know you are tired of fund-raisers, offering pitches, etc.,. . .so sit back, take off your shoes, relax, and have a cup of tea on us." In each envelope you place a tea bag. Also ask the church member, "While you are relaxing, we'd like you to think about your youth group and consider helping them with their special project. . .(etc., etc.)." Casually ask for a donation, but make it as soft sell as possible. One group raised $800 with this approach and got many compliments.

THIRTY PIECES OF SILVER

If you are raising funds around Easter, it would be appropriate to ask people to give "thirty pieces of silver" (dimes, quarters, silver dollars, etc.) in a special offering. Each person should bring the money on Easter Sunday (or Palm Sunday) as a reminder of the thirty pieces of silver that were used in the betrayal of Jesus Christ. You can emphasize that this provides the opportunity to symbolically put thirty pieces of silver to work for the kingdom rather than in opposition to it.

UGLY CONTEST

Here's a fund-raiser with a sense of humor. Line up several people in your church who are willing to compete in an "Ugly Contest" (the opposite of a "Beauty Contest"). Each contestant should have their photo taken (in as ugly a pose as possible) and then the photos can be displayed above a jar or box that can accept money. Members of the church are then invited to "vote" for their favorite candidate by depositing money in the receptacle. You can make this even more fun by encouraging "campaigning" on the part of the candidates and their supporters, "stuffing the ballot box," and so on. Make sure all your "ugly candidates" are volunteers, and make sure that everyone knows that the money collected is going to an important service project.

WORLD HUNGER BANQUET

This event will raise money for world hunger and will also raise the consciousness of the group regarding world hunger. Plan a banquet and program and invite everyone to attend. The food should be served buffet-style, with the following entrees spread out on a table with signs indicating the price of each item. It should be explained to everyone that they can order their choice of food, but they may NOT EXCEED thirteen cents, which represents the daily food budget of most of the world's population. They pick up their food and pay the cashier at the end of the table.

Menu

Water — 1¢	Olives — 2¢ each
Coffee — 6¢ a cup	Orange slices — 8¢ each
Sugar — 2¢	Hard-boiled eggs — 6¢ each
Milk — 2¢	Carrots — 3¢ a serving
Saltines — 1¢ each	Sweet pickles — 2¢ a serving
American cheese — 6¢	Raisins — 9¢ a serving
Radishes — 1¢ a serving	Cookies — 3¢ each

Following the meal itself, you can lead a discussion concerning the problem of world hunger, and ask everyone to become personally involved. You might suggest (for starters) that people give the difference between what they paid for their meal (13 cents) and what they might have paid for a regular meal at a restaurant. Of course, some people will want to give more. The money can then be sent to an agency that is working to fight world hunger.

Chapter Seven

Agencies and Organizations Committed to Social Action

This chapter lists selected organizations committed to various kinds of social action. It is by no means an exhaustive list, but then an exhaustive list of anything usually winds up being counter-productive. There are many organizations that could have been included in this chapter, but we have tried to include those with which we are familiar and which have something specific to offer youth groups. Hopefully, you will find this list adequate and useful.

Addresses and phone numbers have been included, even though phone numbers have a tendency to change frequently. Use them at your own risk. A brief description of each organization is provided to help you decide whether or not it will meet your needs.

Almost all of the organizations listed here are supported by contributions. If your group is interested in raising funds for social action, then you might consider supporting one of them. Of course, it is always recommended that you examine carefully the ministry and financial responsibility of any organization that you choose to support.

AMERICAN RED CROSS
Youth Services
National Headquarters
Washington, D.C. 20006

The Red Cross has become an American institution, and its activities all over the world are well-known. Its "Youth Services" division provides a way for youth groups to become active members of the Red Cross and to assist in a variety of projects. The Red Cross will provide training for your young people in areas like alcohol abuse, consumer survival skills, first aid, health and safety, and recreation. There are also volunteer opportunities provided by the Red Cross for services within the local community. Examples include working at bloodmobiles, serving on "Disaster Action Teams," working in hospitals, homes for the elderly, day-care centers, and other community agencies. By contacting the local chapter of the American Red Cross, you can get specific information regarding the programs available in your community.

AMNESTY INTERNATIONAL
National Office   212/582-4440 East Coast
304 West 58th Street   213/388-1237 West Coast
New York, NY 10019

A recipient of the Nobel Peace Prize in 1977, Amnesty International is ". . .a worldwide movement of people working for the release of prisoners of conscience. for fair trials for political prisoners, and for an end to torture and the death penalty." The organization invites volunteers to join "adoption groups," "campus network groups," to write letters, to work with "action networks," and more. This organization can help sensitize your group to the needs of oppressed and suffering people all over the world. An annual membership in Amnesty International costs $12 for students, $20 for adults.

AMOR INDUSTRIES
Aiding Mexican Orphanages and Refugees
2500 E. Nutwood Ave., Ste. 121A
Fullerton, CA 92631
(714) 680-6402

AMOR is an evangelical mission agency with ministries in Mexico and inner cities of the U.S. It provides cross-cultural opportunities in which youth groups and individuals may serve during the summer, vacations and on weekends. Projects include building (churches, homes and orphanages), distribution of food and clothing, and organizing both ministerial and recreational activities with the children. If you have been looking for a way to get your youth group involved in a mission trip to Mexico, this organization can set it up for you. There are no fees required, only the group's willingness to work and to serve others. AMOR also has a "sponsor an orphan" program. Write or call them for details.

APPALACHIA SERVICE PROJECT
Asbury Center
Boone and Watauga
Johnson City, TN 37601
(615) 928-1776

The Appalachia Service Project is a "home repair project" affiliated with the United Methodist Church. The organization was founded in 1969, and since then has repaired well over 3,000 homes in the poorest

regions of Kentucky and Tennessee. While it is affiliated with the United Methodist Church, it is an independent, non-profit corporation that will involve any youth group in its ministry, regardless of denominational ties. Youth groups can send a team to be involved in the work of the Appalachia Service Project by writing to the address above and asking for an application.

BREAD FOR THE WORLD
6411 Chillum Place N.W.
Washington, D.C. 20012
(202) 722-4100

Bread for the World is "a Christian Citizen's Movement" that was formed by Arthur Simon to help enact public policy and legislation that is in the best interests of the poor and needy of the world. BFW does not do any food distribution itself, but attempts to sensitize individuals, government leaders, and others to hunger needs around the world. Members of Bread for the World receive a monthly bulletin informing them of pending legislation that is relevant to hunger issues so that they may write their congresspersons and ask them to vote the right way. Bread for the World has had a major impact on much legislation that provides food for hungry people, both at home and abroad. Churches and youth groups are invited to join and to become a part of this large network of people across America who are concerned about hunger.

CARE
660 First Avenue
New York, NY 10016
(212) 686-3110

CARE is probably the largest relief agency in the world, having provided over three billion dollars in aid to people in over 80 countries since it was founded in 1946. The "CARE package" has become a household word. Its goals today are the same: to feed the hungry, to provide emergency aid, to establish self-help programs, and to offer health assistance to the poor and needy all over the world. Part of the organization's success has to do with its efficiency and skill at getting things done. (96% of its funds goes directly to the field.) There are regional CARE offices all over the United States and Canada, so if you are interested in working with CARE, write the national office (above address) for the brochure "The What and Where of CARE" for regional information. If your group is involved in a hunger project, CARE has a number of films and other resources that you might find useful. CARE is funded, like most relief organizations, solely by contributions.

CATHOLIC RELIEF SERVICES
1011 First Avenue
New York, NY 10022
(212) 838-4700

This is the major relief agency of the U.S. Catholic Church, serving the poor of over 70 countries without regard to race or creed. Its aim is to meet the needs of the poor with programs to encourage better nutrition, healthier children and a greater sense of self-determination. CRS annually channels more than 350 million dollars into development assistance to Third World countries, emergency aid and disaster relief, help for orphans, the aged, the handicapped and the seriously ill, refugee aid, and other programs. CRS is supported by the Catholic Church, government aid, grants and individual donors.

CHILDREN'S DEFENSE FUND

1520 New Hampshire Avenue, N.W.
Washington, D.C. 20036
(202) 483-1470

The Children's Defense Fund is a lot more than just a "fund." It is an organization that exists to provide a strong and effective voice for the children of America who cannot vote, lobby, or speak for themselves when critical policy decisions are made that affect their lives. The goal of the organization is to educate the nation about the needs of children and to encourage preventive investment in children before they get sick, drop out of school, or get into trouble. Of particular interest to CDF are poor, minority, and handicapped children. CDF has published a number of pamphlets and other resources for groups who are interested in children. Their "Children's Sabbath Packet" offers a wealth of program and worship ideas for churches who want to raise issues concerning child welfare. If your group wants to become involved in a ministry on behalf of children, then the Children's Defense Fund can be a valuable resource.

CHURCH WORLD SERVICES

National Council of the Churches of Christ in the U.S.A.
475 Riverside Drive
Room 620
New York, NY 10115

Church World Service is the relief and development arm of the National Council of Churches. It is one link in a worldwide network of U.S. churches and overseas agencies working in partnership to "help people help themselves." CWS represents 31 Protestant and Orthodox churches and works in cooperation with colleague agencies in 74 countries. Through this network, human and material resources are channelled to people in need in every part of the world.

Seventeen Protestant denominations organized CWS in 1946 in the aftermath of World War II to offer help to people caught in disasters and related events of critical need. Today, CWS has expanded its concern to include development programs which address the causes of suffering and make it possible for people to determine the course of their own lives.

Programs sponsored by CWS include: well digging and irrigation projects, food production, child care, education, housing, vocational training, technological development, disaster relief and refugee resettlement.

Associated with CWS is another organization known as "CROP." CROP is the way in which CWS raises funds for world hunger. Like similar agencies, CROP sponsors a hunger fast program for youth groups and individuals designed to raise money for the poor, as well as a "Walk for the Hungry" and a variety of other events.

COMPASSION INTERNATIONAL

P.O. Box 7000
Colorado Springs, CO 80933
(303) 594-9900

Compassion International is a 33 year old relief and educational ministry founded by Rev. Everett Swanson in Korea to aid orphans and refugees in that war torn country. Today, Compassion co-labors with more than sixty evangelical church and mission organizations and sponsors over 70,000 children in more than 30 countries.

CROP

28606 Phillips Street
Elkhart, IN 46515
(219) 264-3102

See "Church World Service" for information on CROP. While CROP has a separate office and staff, it is affiliated with CWS.

EVANGELICAL ASSOCIATION FOR THE PROMOTION OF EDUCATION

P.O. Box 238
St. Davids, PA 19087
(215) 293-0780

E.A.P.E. is a non-profit corporation founded in 1967 by Tony Campolo. It is involved in educational, medical and economic programs in the Dominican Republic, Haiti and Niger, as well as work in the inner city here in the United States. E.A.P.E. is based at Eastern College in St. David's, PA, and can provide opportunities to work in the inner city of Philadelphia during the summer months. Young people willing to pay their own way may also participate in work projects in Third World nations. E.A.P.E. has set up an orphanage in Haiti and can utilize financial gifts to sponsor children in need in the Third World. Write or call for information.

EVANGELICALS FOR SOCIAL ACTION

P.O. Box 76560
Washington, D.C. 20013
703/237-7464

Founded in 1978 by Ronald Sider, ESA is a national movement of evangelicals committed to "dynamic Biblical justice." The organization offers its members the resources they need to become meaningfully informed and actively involved in such issues as peace, nuclear disarmament, abortion, poverty, the family, racial and sex discrimination, human rights, protection of the environment, and others. Members of ESA receive a monthly newsletter with articles and commentary from evangelical leaders as well as creative ideas for local community projects. ESA also publishes a number of tracts and pamphlets of many of the issues with which they are concerned, and they sponsor "Discipleship Workshops" all over the country.

FOOD FOR THE HUNGRY

7729 East Greenway Road
Scottsdale, AZ 85260
602/955-8438

Food for the Hungry was started in 1971 by Dr. Larry Ward as a nonprofit, nondenominational organization committed to disaster relief and long-range, self-help assistance to the poor of the world. Food for the Hungry solicits funds which are used for these programs and also enlists volunteers who work overseas in their "Hunger Corps." This program is for adults who are 21 or over. In addition, Food for the Hungry has a child sponsorship program called "Everychild."

GROUP MAGAZINE WORKCAMPS

P.O. Box 431
Loveland, Colorado 80539

Every summer, Group magazine organizes several workcamps in both inner-city and rural locations around the country. Youth groups are then invited to participate and "give a week of your summer to show God's love to a needy family." Young people pay their own expenses plus a registration fee. Group does all the rest.

HOLT INTERNATIONAL CHILDREN'S SERVICES, INC.
P.O. Box 2880
Eugene, OR 97402
(503) 687-2202

This organization is one of the world's leading international adoption agencies. Founded twenty-six years ago, Holt International maintains orphanages, provides emergency shelter and health care, nutritional and emotional rehabilitation, and ultimately permanent homes to abandoned and otherwise endangered children in Korea, Vietnam, the Philippines, Thailand, Nicaragua, and India. Although the organization is best known as an adoption agency, it also provides care for children through a child sponsorship program. Through this program, people may support children who, because of handicaps or other difficulties, may never be adopted. Brochures are available from Holt on all of their programs and services. It is a nondenominational Christian organization.

INTERCRISTO: The Christian Career Specialists
A division of CRISTA Ministries
P.O. Box 33487
19303 Fremont Avenue North
Seattle, WA 98133
1-800-426-1343 toll free (Alaska, Hawaii, Washington state (206) 546-7330)

Intercristo is a nonprofit ministry which matches Christians with job opportunities in Christian organizations. Christians in the U.S. and Canada are eligible to use Intercristo's services. Approximately 1,000 Christian organizations list jobs in the U.S. and overseas. They include denominations, international missions, churches, camps, social service agencies, media ministries and schools. There are often more than 25,000 job openings on file.

If you have young people who are looking for a place where they can use their talents and abilities in a ministry position, have them contact Intercristo. Some of the openings are paid positions, others are volunteer positions.

INTER-FAITH CENTER FOR CORPORATE RESPONSIBILITY

475 Riverside Drive, Room 566
New York, NY 10027
(212) 870-2293

Here's an organization that can help your youth group to get involved in international concerns. This nondenominational agency collects reliable information about corporations whose activities in Third World countries are essentially destructive and evil from the Christian point of view. This organization is associated with the National Council of Churches, and they will not only provide you with information on almost any major corporation that you wish to know about, but they will also suggest possible courses of action for your youth group to effect positive change. You may want to get your group involved in a letter-writing campaign, or in negotiations, or any number of things to make American business leaders more accountable to God for their actions.

JONI AND FRIENDS

P.O. Box 3225
Woodland Hills, CA 91365
(213) 348-5556

This organization was founded by Joni Eareckson Tada, the well-known paraplegic who has inspired millions through her books and the film about her life. Joni and Friends is a ministry to "those who suffer," more specifically, to those who are handicapped. The organization publishes curriculum and other resource material for use in churches and youth groups to help people to become more aware of the needs of the handicapped. The organization also sponsors JAF Seminars in various cities around the country and produces a syndicated radio program. If your group is considering a ministry to the handicapped, Joni and Friends can provide you with some excellent resources.

JUBILEE FUND

300 West Apsley Street
Philadelphia, PA 19144
215/849-0770

Jubilee Fund was established by *The Other Side* magazine to provide financial resources for selected projects all over the world that are helping to fight the causes of oppression, starvation, and poverty. These projects range from helping to improve labor conditions among exploited workers in Hong Kong to training women for the Christian ministry in Latin America. A related ministry of *The Other Side* magazine is Jubilee Crafts, which sells Third World crafts to people in the West. This allows poor people to help themselves instead of being forced to starve or take handouts. Perhaps your youth group could help to market these craft products. A brochure is available which describes these ministries in detail.

KAIROS ASSOCIATES
1088 Goodrich Avenue
St. Paul, MN 55105
(612) 222-2319

This organization was set up to provide a base of operation for a number of Christians who minister to the poor around the world. Your contributions can either be designated to go into a general fund which finances administrative costs and long-term projects, or, to a specific ministry where 100% of what you give goes directly to the poor and needy in Third World countries.

For example, Kairos sponsors evangelist Thoma Daniel in Sri Lanka. His life is devoted to sharing God's love to the outcasts in his country. Thoma's orphanage and prison ministry is much like Mother Teresa's in that he lives on an income comparable to those he is ministering to. The complete amount of any check earmarked for Thoma will go directly for food, medicine and clothing, and nothing more.

LOS NINOS
1333 Continental St.
San Ysidro, CA 92073
(619) 690-1437

Los Ninos (pronounced NEEN-yohs) is a grass roots, interfaith organization that attempts to reach out to poor children, primarily in Mexico. Ninos is the Spanish word for "little ones," and Los Ninos does whatever it can to help the little ones of Mexico. The organization provides financial resources to numerous orphanages, as well as food, medicine, carpenters, teachers, and much more. Los Ninos also sponsors World Hunger Seminars, annual "Tortilla Marathons" (a 250 mile walk for hunger), and "Supermarket Stake-outs" to gather food for the poor. Los Ninos would be an excellent organization with which to work on a hunger project, especially if your youth group is in the southwestern United States.

MEALS FOR MILLIONS
815 Second Ave., Suite 1001
New York, NY 10017
(212) 986-4170

Meals for Millions is a nonprofit organization fighting hunger and malnutrition through programs which aim to strengthen the capabilities of developing communities to solve their own food and nutrition problems. It is supported by contributions from the general public.

MENNONITE CENTRAL COMMITTEE
21 South Twelfth Street
Akron, PA 17501
(717) 859-1151

The Mennonite Central Committee is the international service and relief agency of the Mennonite and Brethern in Christ churches in the United States and Canada. MCC has over 750 personnel serving two to three-year assignments in agriculture, economic and technical development, education, health, and social services in about 45 countries overseas and in Noth America.

The ministries of MCC are performed in the name of Christ and arise in response to human need and the call to Christian discipleship. The program uses personnel with a wide variety of skills, backgrounds and levels of education and maturity. MCC seeks workers who are Christians, active participants in a Christian church, and committed to a lifestyle of peacemaking. They need not be Mennonite, but should be able to endorse the traditional Mennonite understanding of peacemaking, which is more than, but includes, pacifism.

The MCC has available a number of informative brochures that describe the many opportunities the organization provides. Write them for a packet of materials and an application form.

MOUNTAIN T.O.P. (Tennessee Outreach Project)
P.O. Box 128
Altamont, TN 37301
(615) 692-3999

Mountain T.O.P. is a Christian mission program designed for youth groups to increase their social awareness while meeting the needs of others. Two summer programs are operated in the Tennessee Cumberland Mountain area of the Southern Appalachias: the Service Project and the Day Camp ministry. After a time of home preparation and study, youth groups come to one of several base camps in the Cumberlands for either a week of involvement in home repair for mountain families or for leading a Day Camp program for mountain children. Mountain T.O.P. is a program agency of the United Methodist Church, but they invite all Christian youth groups to participate with them.

NATIONAL COMMISSION ON RESOURCES FOR YOUTH

605 Commonwealth Avenue
Boston, MA 02215
(617) 353-3309

The National Commission on Resources for Youth collects information about outstanding service projects for adolescents, catalogues it, and disseminates it to schools and other youth-serving agencies that wish to start or to improve projects. NCRY also provides training conferences and technical assistance. They make available many printed and audio-visual materials that describe outstanding service projects and give principles that must be applied when doing them. Write for a catalog of their publications and services

OXFAM AMERICA

115 Broadway
Boston, MA 02116
(617) 482-1211

Oxfam America is an international agency that funds self-help development projects and disaster relief in poor countries in Asia, Africa, and Latin America, and also prepares and distributes educational materials for Americans on issues of development and hunger. The name "Oxfam" came from the Oxford Committee for Famine Relief, founded in England in 1942. Oxfam America, based in Boston, was formed in 1970 and is one of six autonomous Oxfams around the world. It is a nonprofit agency, and seeks contributions to further its work.

PRACTICAL MISSIONARY TRAINING

8625 La Prada Drive
Dallas, TX 75228
(214) 327-8206

Practical Missionary Training (PMT) is a ministry of CAM International (Central American Mission) which was founded by C. I. Scofield. PMT trains young adults to work on the mission field, both in evangelism and service, and also provides opportunities for on-the-field training in Mexico, Central America and Spain. PMT also has an Easter week program in Guadalajara, Mexico, for high school students who want to participate in a mission experience.

PRISON FELLOWSHIP
P.O. Box 40562
Washington, D.C. 20016
(703) 759-9401 or 759-4521

Chuck Colson, following his own prison term in the aftermath of the Watergate Conspiracy, founded Prison Fellowship in 1976 to provide hope and Christian friendship to inmates all over the United States. The organization is active in the prison reform movement and can provide churches and youth groups with literature and ideas on how to become more involved in prison reform. Prison Fellowship has nearly 150 "Care Committees" across the country and a staff of over 30 state and regional directors working in both federal and state institutions. Prison Fellowship can help youth groups and church groups who are interested in prison ministry by providing resources, contacts, and ideas. Prison Fellowship is supported solely by contributions.

SALVATION ARMY
National Headquarters
799 Bloomfield Avenue
Verona,NJ 07044
(201) 239-0606

This organization is a well-known Christian social service agency which assists the poor and does important evangelistic work all over the world. Services include the operation of inner-city missions and churches, family counseling, summer camps, financial aid to the needy, senior citizens' programs, drug and alcohol rehabilitation programs, homes for unwed mothers, and much more. The local Salvation Army in your area can provide suggestions on how your young people can become involved in their ongoing ministry.

SPECTRUM MINISTRIES

3286 Erie Street
San Diego, CA 92117
(619) 276-1963

This organization was set up to provide a base of operation for Pastor E. G. Von Trutschler who has worked for many years with the poor of Mexico and other countries to the south. He has been involved in youth ministry, both in the U.S. and abroad, for over thirty years. Von's ministry now includes mission work, speaking, training youth workers, relief work, and camping ministries. If you want to get your youth group involved in service, Spectrum Ministries can offer advice, direction, and assistance.

TEEN MISSIONS INTERNATIONAL

P.O. Box 1056
Merritt Island, FL 32952
(305) 453-0350

Teen Missions is a nondenominational organization that sends teams of high school and college-age students all over the world on mission trips. They work in cooperation with local missionaries, world relief organizations, and many denominations to find ways for American young people to "get dirty for God" by doing work projects out on the mission field. Teen Missions sets everything up — the project, the transportation, the supplies and the leadership. They invite youth groups or individual teens to sign up for a wide variety of projects, both at home and abroad. To date, more than 365 teams have served in 48 countries since the organization was founded in 1971.

Teen Missions provides transportation from various locations around the U.S. to its "boot camp" in Florida where the young people are trained before leaving for the mission field. After the work project has been finished, the kids return for a "debriefing" period, which is vitally important to the process of learning and understanding the significance of what they have done. Each project requires that the young people raise their own support to handle costs, the amount of which depends on the particular project. Teen Missions provides helpful material for the young people to use in their fund-raising drive. If your group is interested in spending a summer (or a good portion of one) serving Christ by helping others, Teen Missions can set it up and insure that the experience will be a good one for you.

TOM SKINNER ASSOCIATES, INC.
505 Eighth Avenue
New York, NY 10018
(212) 563-5454

Tom Skinner Associates, Inc., is a nonprofit organization which ministers to all people in general, but to black people in particular. The ministries of the organization include work on inner-city streets, in state prisons, and on predominately black college campuses such as Norfolk State University, Howard University, and others. Other ministries and services include citywide evangelistic crusades and rallies, various teaching institutes, and seminars for pastors and lay leaders. Tom Skinner Associates also sponsors an inner-city youth club program called "Release." A primary aim of the organization is to develop quality leadership within the black community. It is supported by contributions from churches and individuals.

UNICEF

The United Nations Children's Fund
331 East 38th Street
New York, NY 10016
(212) 686-5522

UNICEF directs its work to the essential needs and problems of children, primarily those in the developing world. It was founded in 1946 as an emergency aid organization to help children in Europe after World War II, and it was awarded the Nobel Peace Prize in 1965. UNICEF now works in 112 countries, providing assistance in the planning and design of services for children, delivery of supplies and equipment for those services, and providing workers.

Should you wish to make a contribution to the general fund of UNICEF, the money will be directed to those parts of the world where it is most needed at the time. You may also earmark contributions for a specific developing country or for a specific project. UNICEF also offers opportunities for volunteer service. Interested persons are encouraged to contact either the national or a local office of UNICEF for more information. While UNICEF is not connected with any particular religious group, it is certainly doing the kind of work that merits the enthusiastic support of the Christian Church.

VACATION SAMARITANS

P.O. Box 16797
Portland, OR 97216
(503) 774-5683

This organization began in 1967 in San Diego, and still has a regional office there. It is an interdenominational Christian agency that channels youth groups into cross-cultural service and community action. They specialize in sending youth during Easter, Christmas, and summer vacation on short-term mission trips to places like Mexico, Central America, Jamaica, Alaska, Indian reservations, even China. The youth group must cover its own expenses, but Vacation Samaritans sets up the trip and organizes the project.

Vacation Samaritans also has similar programs for families and single adults. In addition, the organization sponsors weekend medical missions into Mexico and other areas. Affiliated with Vacation Samaritans is "Cycle Samaritans" (bicycle trips), Samaritan Seminars (mission opportunities and travel), and Samaritan Medical Services.

VIISA
Volunteers in International Service and Awareness
P.O. Box 6790
Santa Barbara, CA 93111
(805) 967-9277

VIISA offers the opportunity for volunteers to be trained and to serve in one of several different service projects in the Dominican Republic and Haiti. These short-term projects of from six to eight weeks are in the areas of public health, nutrition, animal husbandry, agriculture, pre-school child development, and reforestation. The program includes a 90-hour home-study course and ten days in a pre-departure orientation seminar. Volunteers need not have specific skills, although knowledge of Spanish or French (Haiti) is helpful. The purpose of the program is to sensitize participants to conditions in the Third World, and to give them the opportunity to live, work, and serve among the poor.

VIISA is a private, nondenominational organization which is endorsed by several church bodies, especially the American Lutheran Church. Youth groups of any church are invited to participate in the projects of VIISA. Information packets are sent on request.

VOICE OF CALVARY MINISTRIES
P.O. Box 10562
Jackson, MS 39209
(601) 353-1635

Voice of Calvary Ministries was founded in 1960 by John Perkins to minister to needy black people in the South. He started a church, then a store and a cooperative farm to help meet the spiritual and material needs of the poor. The organization eventually began to confront unjust political systems and power structures that seemed to be the causes of poverty and racism, and became a major force in the civil rights movement. Today there are a number of projects that come under the umbrella of VOC. Among them are "People's Development, Inc.," a housing cooperative that buys and renovates deteriorating homes, which are then rented or resold to the poor. "Thriftco" is a developing network of thrift stores located in poor areas. Health centers sponsored by VOC bring medical and dental services to both rural and urban areas. The John Perkins International Study Center has been established to train people for work in community development.

VOC also provides opportunities for groups and individuals to come to Jackson and to do volunteer work among the poor. In addition, VOC seeks fund-raising help from youth groups who feel led to support their ministry.

VOLUNTEERS FOR MISSION

Episcopal Church Center
815 Second Avenue
New York, NY 10017
(212) 867-8400

Volunteers for Mission is an agency of the Episcopal Church seeking dedicated people of any age (18 years and older) who want to serve Christ either overseas or at home. VFM attempts to match the skills of the volunteer to the needs of churches and other institutions who are seeking workers. Typical assignments include: assisting in Hispanic ministry in an inner-city parish, experimenting with farming methods and crops, instructing homemakers in hygiene and family planning, assisting in a mobile clinic, and similar ministries. Interested persons are invited to request information at the above address.

VOLUNTEERS IN ACTION

World Gospel Mission
Box W.G.M.
Marion, IN 46952
(317) 664-7331

This organization is, in its own words, "interdenominational, thoroughly evangelistic, Wesleyan in doctrine, cooperating with other evangelical agencies," providing mission opportunities for high school and college students in various locations all over the world. VIA organizes evangelistic crusades and witnessing campaigns during the summer, both in foreign countries and in the U.S., and seeks volunteers to help work in them. If you have young people who are interested in doing evangelistic work or in going to the mission field, this organization can give them some good exposure to that sort of thing at a relatively low cost and with good supervision.

VOLUNTEERS IN MISSION
The United Presbyterian Church
475 Riverside Drive, Room 1126
New York, NY 10115
212/870-2801

This ecumenical organization was established by the United Presbyterian Church to place volunteers in Christian service throughout the U.S. and the world. Their publication, *Voluntary Service Bulletin* lists hundreds of opportunities for service. They invite Christians of all ages, regardless of church affiliation, to respond to any opportunity that interests them. Most require people who are willing to work hard for very little pay. In addition, VIM sponsors an "International Christian Youth Exchange," a Christian ministry in the national parks, and international work camp programs. A brochure is available which will furnish details on all of these.

VOLUNTEER YOUTH MINISTRY
The Lutheran Church—Missouri Synod
1333 South Kirkwood Road
St. Louis, MO 63122
(314) 965-9000

The Lutheran Church — Missouri Synod has a variety of excellent opportunities for Lutheran youth who want to serve in either short or long-term assignments, both at home and overseas. Normally, the overseas assignments are for older youth (college graduates) who can make a commitment of two or three years, but the LCMS organizes many work camps and mission trips in the U.S. for teens who want to work during the summer. These are called "Servant Events" and range from home repair in Appalachia to working with poor Mexican-American children in El Paso, Texas.

WORLD CONCERN
Box 33000
Seattle, WA 98133
(206) 546-7201

World Concern is a Christian humanitarian relief and development agency serving the needs of the poor in Third World countries. World Concern works in relief to assist refugees, and in rehabilitation aid to assist people recovering from disaster. Various self-help and self-reliance projects sponsored by World Concern make it possible for people to help themselves through difficult times. One trademark of World Concern is its reluctance to display its name all over overseas projects. Instead, World Concern works in partnership with mission groups and indigenous national churches which foster the attitude of self-help.

World Concern has a very fine program for youth groups called "Refugee Camp," which is similar to a hunger fast but with a unique twist. During this project, youth groups set up and live in their own simulated Refugee Camp for 24 hours. The youth do without TV, radio, electronic games, and any other gadgets that would not be found in a real refugee camp. This helps young people find enjoyment in simplicity and also it helps them identify with those who have lost everything through war or famine. Participants in World Concern Refugee Camps are forced to create their own fun activities with the simplest of props. Other simulations include a "Boredom Block" (just dealing with boredom for four hours) and a time when a group member "gets sick" but receives no medical attention.

During the Refugee Camp, the young people receive only the same amount of food as a real refugee might get. Food is rationed in small amounts and it is very basic — rice, bread, water. World Concern provides a leader's guide which contains numerous exercises, games, simulations, and discussions which can be used during the Refugee Camp experience. There is also a film called "The Myths of Hunger" which is provided by World Concern.

In addition to the learning that takes place, the Refugee Camp will provide funds to help the poor. Like similar programs, the young people get sponsors who will support them during their Refugee Camp experience. The money that is collected for World Concern goes to fund their hunger and relief projects, especially those that help refugees in real refugee camps. The youth group can keep up to 50% of the money for projects of their own choosing. World Concern provides all the supplies, films, posters, sponsor sheets, leader's guides, and so on. It's one of the best programs of its kind.

World Concern also sponsors "Runs for Hunger" (a youth jog-a-thon event), "Share Crates" (a collection bank program), speakers and other resources on world hunger. Write or phone the World Concern office for further details.

WORLD RELIEF
P.O. Box WRC
Wheaton, IL 60187
(312) 665-0235 or (800) 431-2808

World Relief is the international relief and development arm of the National Association of Evangelicals (NAE). Since its founding in 1945, World Relief has been involved in disaster relief and rehabilitation, self-help programs to combat hunger and poverty, and refugee resettlement. In fact, World Relief is the largest Christian refugee resettlement agency in the United States. Its Refugee Services Division (RSD) was established to help refugees who have been approved for resettlement in the United States find a sponsor and then insure a successful resettlement by assisting both the refugee and the sponsor in this country.

World Relief's Refugee Services Division has been able to help refugees from almost every continent on earth. To date, they have resettled over 36,000 refugees from Indochina (Vietnam, Cambodia, and Laos), Cuba, Haiti, Afghanistan, Africa, and Eastern Europe.

World Relief encourages youth groups to become involved in the ministry of helping refugees, and the organization will provide ideas and resources upon request. In addition, World Relief sponsors an overseas volunteer program for students called "Open Hands" which sends teams of young people into areas of the world where there is great need. Participants in this program may receive up to three semester hours of academic credit through a program offered by Eastern College in St. Davids, Pennsylvania, under the supervision of Dr. Campolo. Brochures on this program are available from World Relief.

WORLD VISION
Box O
Monrovia, CA 91016
(213) 357-1111 or (800) 423-3366 toll free

World Vision is a Christian humanitarian agency which has become well-known for its work all over the world. World Vision has been a pioneer in famine and disaster relief, refugee resettlement, and the establishment of missions, schools and orphanages in Third World countries. A primary focus of World Vision is evangelism and the development of self-reliance in poor nations, as well as emergency aid. World Vision now operates programs in 85 countries.

World Vision offers an excellent program for youth groups called "Planned Famine" in which young people fast for 30 hours to help hungry people. Since the program was created in 1977, youth groups around the U.S. have raised more than 2.5 million dollars to fight hunger in the name of Christ. The Planned Famine program is a great way to raise funds as well as to educate young people concerning the plight of the poor and needy.

World Vision's Planned Famine program is not only well-conceived, but packaged in such a way as to make it easy for groups to participate. Everything needed for a Planned Famine is provided by World Vision. They will provide a free 16mm film called "Let It Growl," which shows an actual group participating in a Planned Famine. It's a good film and a great way to get your group motivated. World Vision also provides a detailed leader's manual, an activity book, resource materials, printed envelopes, sponsor sign-up sheets, thank you notes, posters, and more. There are even "Let-It-Growl" t-shirts available if you want them.

The money is raised by each individual giving $6.00 of his or her own money (what they would normally spend on food for the 30-hour period) and asking sponsors to match it. A youth with ten sponsors would raise a total of $66.00. World Vision allows each group the option of keeping up to 60% of the total for any hunger project it chooses. The balance (or the entire amount) is sent to World Vision for hunger relief. Recently, hundreds of youth groups, in cooperation with Youth Specialties and World Vision, conducted Planned Famines to raise money for a feeding program in Haiti organized by Tony Campolo and E.A.P.E. As one youth worker described it: "The Planned Famine unified our group, gave us a sense of accomplishment, relieved suffering overseas and, I believe, pleased our Lord."

YOUTH WITH A MISSION
P.O. Box 4600
Tyler, TX 75712
(214) 882-5591

This organization was founded in 1960 by Loren Cunningham, and today is probably the largest organization of its kind with more than 100 centers worldwide in over 40 countries. It is nondenominational, and its aim is to channel Christians into mission work. A primary goal of this aggressive organization is world evangelism. YWAM is also involved in what they call "mercy ministries," which includes hunger and disaster relief worldwide. Recently the organization acquired a huge cruise ship which it uses for its training schools and for doing relief work. Volunteers are sought for both short and long-term ministry at home and abroad.

Suggested Reading List

Clapp, Steve. *Repairing Christian Lifestyles: A Manual For Youth.* Sidell, Ill.: C-4 Resources, 1980.

Dayton, Donald W. *Discovering an Evangelical Heritage.* New York: Harper & Row, 1976.

Dieleman, Dale. *Handbook on Service.* Grand Rapids, Mich.: Baker Book House, 1979.

Finnerty, Adam. *No More Plastic Jesus.* Maryknoll, N.Y.: Orbis Books, 1977.

Freund, Ronald. *What One Christian Can Do to Help Prevent Nuclear War.* Chicago: Fides/Claretian, 1982.

Gladwin, John. *God's People in God's World: Biblical Motives for Social Involvement.* Downer's Grove, Ill.: Inter Varsity Press, 1979.

Gremillion, Joseph B. *The Gospel of Peace & Justice.* Maryknoll, N.Y.: Orbis Books, 1976.

Heckman, Shirley. *Peace is Possible.* New York: Pilgram Press, 1982.

Hutchinson, Robert. *Hunger in America.* Chicago: Fides/Claretian, 1982.

Kraybill, Donald B. *The Upside-Down Kingdom.* Scottdale, PA.: Herald Press, 1978.

Lehmann, Paul Louis. *The Transfiguration of Politics.* New York: Harper & Row, 1975.

Longacre, Doris. *More With Less Cookbook.* Scottdale, PA.: Herald Press, 1976.

McClory, Robert J. *Racism in America.* Chicago: Fides/Claretian, 1981.

Moberg, David O. *Inasmuch.* Grand Rapids, Mich.: Eerdmans, 1965.

Mott, Stephen C. *Biblical Ethics & Social Change.* New York: Oxford University Press, 1982.

Mouw, Richard S. *Politics & the Biblical Drama.* Grand Rapids, Mich.: Eerdmans, 1976.

Niebuhr, Reinhold. *Moral Man & Immoral Society.* New York: Scribner, 1960.

Perkins, John. *A Quiet Revolution.* Waco, TX.: World Books, 1976.

Perkins, John. *With Justice for All*. Ventura, CA.: Regal Books, 1982.

Price, Morris D. *Your Need for Bread is Mine: Resources for Helping The Hungry*. New York: Friendship Press, 1977.

Schumacher, E.F. *Small is Beautiful*. New York: Harper & Row, 1973.

Scott, Waldron. *Bring Forth Justice: A Contemporary Perspective on Mission*. Grand Rapids, Mich.: Eerdmans, 1980.

Sider, Ronald S. *Rich Christians in an Age of Hunger*. Downer's Grove, Ill.: Inter Varsity Press, 1977.

Sider, Ronald S. & Taylor, Richard. *Nuclear Holocaust & Christian Hope*. Downer's Grove, Ill.: Inter Varsity Press, 1982.

Sine, Tom. *The Mustard Seed Conspiracy*. Waco, TX.: Word Books, 1981.

Sprinkle, Patricia. *Hunger: Understanding the Crisis through Games, Drama and Songs*. Atlanta: John Knox Press, 1980.

Taylor, John V. *Enough is Enough*. Minneapolis: Augsburg, 1977.

True, Michael. *Homemade Social Justice: Teaching Peace & Justice*. Chicago: Fides/Claretian, 1982.

Van Beilen, Aileen. *Hunger Awareness Dinners*. Scottdale, PA.: Herald Press, 1978.

Wallis, Jim. *Agenda for Biblical People*. New York: Harper & Row, 1976.

Wallis, Jim. *Call to Conversion*. New York: Harper & Row, 1981.

Webber, Robert. *The Secular Saint: A Case for Evangelical Social Responsibility*. Grand Rapids, Mich.: Zondervan, 1979.

Yoder, John Howard. *The Politics of Jesus*. Grand Rapids, Mich.: Eerdmans, 1976.

.